Hq Co 3BN 104th Regt 26 INF DIV

PFC 13146453

Richard D Courtney

Dec 8, 1996

Normandy
to the
Bulge

Normandy to the Bulge

An American Infantry GI in Europe During World War II

Pfc. Richard D. Courtney

With a Foreword by
Lt. Col. William A. Foley Jr.

Southern Illinois University Press
Carbondale & Edwardsville

Library of Congress Cataloging-in-Publication Data

Courtney, Richard D., 1925–
    Normandy to the Bulge : an American infantry GI in Europe during
    World War II / Richard D. Courtney : with a foreword by William A. Foley, Jr.
        p.   cm.
    Includes index.
    1. Courtney, Richard D., 1925–   . 2. World War, 1939–1945—
Campaigns—Western Front. 3. World War, 1939–1945—Personal
narratives, American. 4. Soldiers—United States—Biography.
5. United States. Army—Biography. I. Title.
D756.C68   1997
940.54'21—dc20   96-7731
ISBN 0-8093-2084-3 (cloth : alk. paper)   CIP

Frontispiece: Studio photograph of Pfc. Richard D. Courtney on furlough at
Altoona, Pennsylvania, January 1944.

The paper used in this publication meets the minimum requirements of American
National Standard for Information Sciences—Permanence of Paper for Printed
Library Materials, ANSI Z39.48-1984. ♾

*This true story is dedicated to all my fellow infantrymen
who did not come back, especially
Martin Agnew and Lambert Ciancaglini.*

Contents

Illustrations

Foreword

This volume is a firsthand account of small-unit combat in America's biggest war. It is based on the original diary of then-Pfc. Richard D. Courtney. It traces in vivid language and detail the advance of United States Army forces, specifically the 26th Infantry Division, from its arrival in Cherbourg through its push to the Rhine and on to the German surrender. The men of the 104th Infantry Regiment of the 26th Infantry Division, in which Courtney was a soldier, are remembered and their deeds brought back to life while focusing on the largest land battle of World War II's western front, the Battle of the Bulge.

John Keegan, in his excellent one-volume history of World War II entitled *The Second World War*, dramatically states that this global conflict was "the largest single event in human history, fought across six of the world's seven continents and all of its oceans." He continues, "It killed fifty million human beings, left hundreds of millions of others wounded in mind or body and materially devastated much of the heartland of civilization." Private Courtney and his fellow Yankee Division soldiers fought to defeat Nazi Germany and liberate its conquests.

In the war for western Europe, America started slowly and finished as the strongest military power on the face of the earth. Hitler's war machine began with over a hundred divisions and the United States with virtually none ready for deployment. Yet with the refitting of Regular Army divisions and the calling up and mobilization of Army National Guard and Army Reserve divisions, the United States would end World War II with nearly a hundred divisions. Truly the "sleeping giant had been awakened."

By the design of President Franklin D. Roosevelt and Prime Minister Winston Churchill, the war in Europe would be fought in phases and would be given priority over the Pacific theater and also over the China-Burma-India campaign. While the United States was mobilizing, England would carry the burden of the new Atlantic Alliance. Over the winter of 1941–42 with war supply and the Battle of the Atlantic in full swing, American forces began deploying for combat in

what Churchill like to call "the soft under belly." This would lead to
the North African, Mediterranean, and ill-fated Italian campaigns. The
last was designed to cause the Germans to recall divisions from Hitler's
marvelous blunder, Operation Barbarossa, the invasion of Russia that
began in June 1941, thus causing the Germans to fight a two-front
war. Although it did not, the Italian campaign nonetheless got the
Allies on the Continent and helped set the stage for a cross-Channel
invasion from England.

In the States, American forces were readying for this attack, which
would be called Operation Overlord and which would become the
largest air-sea invasion in the history of the world. Although much
debated and delayed, when launched on June 6, 1944, it sent American infantry forces into Normandy, France, to end Hitler's Third Reich.
It would then take most of June and July to expand the beachhead
with the breakout taking place at the very end of July in Operation
Cobra. For the breakout, many follow-on forces would be needed and
they, after being trained in the United States, were on their way into
the European theater in August 1944, to land at Cherbourg. They
would help lead the push into Germany, and one of these units was the
26th Yankee Division of the Massachusetts National Guard.

The enlisted men's story is best told by Courtney in this volume.
After helping defeat the most serious threat to this nation's survival
since the Civil War, the surviving men of the 104th Infantry Regiment
would now help, in various occupations, build post–World War II
America. After their homeward voyage across the Atlantic, they would
begin a new life, free from the threat of Nazi Germany. Not everyone
would be there. There would be many "empty chairs."

The 104th Infantry Regiment had lost 663 who died in combat
and 35 who were listed as "missing in action." A total of 2,174 were
wounded by enemy action, and 401 were injured while serving in the
combat zone.

The 104th Infantry became one of the most highly decorated units
of World War II. Adding to its long line of battle streamers, which
ranged from Boston and Bennington in the Revolutionary War, through
Chancellorsville, Fredericksburg, Gettysburg, and the Wilderness in
the Civil War, plus those from the Spanish-American War and World
War I, would be five new ones. These would be Northern France, the
Rhineland, Ardennes, Central Europe, and the Combat Infantry
Streamer.

Eleven men of the 104th Regiment earned the Distinguished Service Cross, more than any other regiment in the 26th Division, with

one man receiving an Oak Leaf Cluster as a second-time award; 350 men were awarded the Silver Star, with seven men receiving Oak Leaf Clusters; 989 men received the Bronze Star Medal with 42 men getting Oak Leaf Clusters.

In addition, several French and Russian medals were awarded. The 104th Regiment received the Croix de Guerre from France for liberating Alsace-Lorraine. The 104th also received this award from France in World War I.

In combat operations, the 104th Regiment captured 19,835 German prisoners and, in addition, trapped 35,000 enemy troops between the 104th and Russian lines at the close of the war.

All of the above-mentioned statistics are from two books that are well worth reading. These are *History of a Combat Regiment, 1639–1945: 104th Infantry* and *The History of the 26th Yankee Division, 1917–1919, 1941–1945*. The first book was written by Pfc. Henry Parrott in 1945, and the second was published by the Yankee Division Veterans Association and printed in Salem, Massachusetts, in 1955.

I conclude by paraphrasing from the 104th Regimental History. Only in the less violent perspective of history is it possible to begin to evaluate the worth of the infantryman, whether rifleman or unit commander. I would add that only in reflection about the past can we now see the importance of the men's sacrifice under hostile fire, in the rain, snow, and mud of fifty years ago on battlefields far away. We thank every one of them for their service to our country.

William A. Foley Jr., Ph.D.
Lieutenant Colonel, Infantry

Preface

At a Kiwanis luncheon in June of 1994, Col. Bill Foley and I were discussing the fiftieth anniversary of the D-Day invasion of Normandy, France. I mentioned that I had been in Normandy with the 26th Infantry Division and all across Europe to Czechoslovakia, including the Battle of the Bulge. He talked about some books he had read about the war in Europe and asked me if I had ever written anything about my experiences during World War II.

I mentioned that I had a set of diary notes kept during the war with the intention of someday writing a book. He asked if he could read my notes, so I made them available to him. A week later we met again, and he said I should expand my notes into a book with the story of an infantry GI.

With his encouragement and my long-buried desire to write such a book, I set about to do it. Little did I realize then how long it would take and how much time I would devote to research and to establishing contacts with my former platoon mates.

It turned out to be an advantage to have been raised in a large family during the Depression, when we learned never to throw anything away because you might need it someday. As a result I hunted through boxes in the attic, bureau drawers, and closet shelves and found pictures and even negatives of pictures taken fifty years ago.

Somehow I had the presence of mind to encase newspapers such as the *YD Grapevine*, our division newspaper, in plastic, which preserved them so well. My mother had even saved my letters sent home from my time in the Army. All of these mementos were invaluable to me in writing my book.

My wife, Connie, and sons Rick, Pat, Tim, Chris, Peter, and Kelly plus my daughter Colleen were all very supportive and enthusiastic boosters of my project. Kelly entered the Order of St. Benedict as a novice at St. Meinrad Archabbey in Indiana at the time I started to write and told his mother that he would pray that Dad would have the patience to finish the book.

Another son, Chris, a captain in the United States Army, had just returned from duty in Germany and was stationed at Fort Huachuca, Arizona. He and his wife, Jené, also a captain, volunteered to type my manuscript into their computer and send me printout sheets.

Since I cannot type, I set about with several ballpoint pens and a pack of tablets to write. After I would compose about thirty pages, I would make copies and mail them to Chris and Jené in Arizona. Not only did they type them, but they also verified my German-language quotes, since they had each spent four years in Germany on duty with the Army.

My family is spread all over the United States and they all called regularly to see how the book was coming and to encourage me to continue. My own brothers and sisters also voiced their support in letters and phone calls.

After the manuscript was edited and rewritten, since Chris and Jené were transferred by the Army to New Jersey, Tim volunteered to do the rewrite on his computer, which he did in Chicago. My son Pat did all the letters of transmittal. Jim Simmons at Southern Illinois University Press used to comment on my "staff" of sons.

Chris and Jené, upon their return to Arizona, got the final and toughest part of the whole book-writing process—helping with the final editing and indexing of the completed manuscript. What a job!

I am so grateful for Chris and Jené, Tim, and Pat, and all their work, and for my friend Bill Foley and his support, and to all my family and friends for their encouragement. Here then is my lifetime dream, the true story of the average American infantry GI in combat in Europe during World War II.

*Normandy
to the
Bulge*

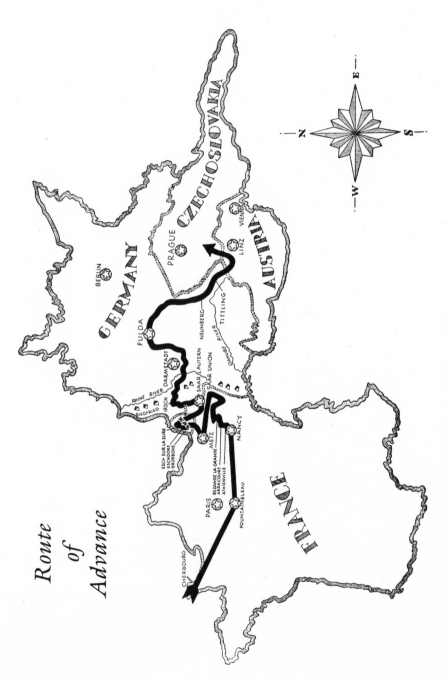

Route of advance of the 104th Infantry Regiment of the 26th Infantry Division. From *History of a Combat Regiment, 1639–1945: 104th Infantry* (1945).

Down the Hill
and
Over the Pond

"AT EASE! GIVE ME YOUR ATTENTION!" It was Capt. Lloyd Nobles, our company commander, grinning at us as we stood in formation on our company street at Camp Shanks, New York, on August 26, 1944. We had just returned from supper when the whistle called us out front.

"At last our training days are over. Tonight is the night. We hit the gangplank at long last. Every man go back into the barracks, gather up all your gear, and fall back out here at 8:00 P.M. sharp. Don't be late because we won't wait."

A shout and a muffled roar arose as we exuberantly burst back into our barracks. "How about that! Tonight! Old 'Gangplank' really means it this time." Lt. Gen. Willard Stuart Paul, our division commander, had been nicknamed "Gangplank" by the men of the 26th Infantry Division because so many times he had promised we were going over and we didn't go.

There was a mad race for a last visit to the latrine, then grunting and groaning as we stuffed our gear into our packs, checked our weapons, and hitched on our gas masks, cartridge belts, canteens, bayonets, full packs, and steel helmets. We were in winter OD uniforms and canvas leggings.

We were all tingling with anticipation and everyone was in a jovial mood. Guys were even being nice to Sergeant Obermeyer, who usually got only derision.

Sgt. Julius T. Obermeyer had been promoted to squad leader, we all thought, because he was big, loud, and muscular. Nobody liked him very much because he was so crude in language and always such a know-it-all. The guys called him Obey for short.

"Are you really going to go, Obey?" someone asked.

"Hey! They can't win this war without me. They are just finding that out," Obey shouted back in his loud raucous voice.

"Pinky" Piquette, our platoon sergeant stood at the door and quietly said, "OK men. Let's go. Everyone outside. Be sure to bring all your gear because we aren't coming back."

Banging into each other, we stumbled down the front steps of the barracks as we also had to drag our full barracks bag, called a B bag, along. We each had a full load.

It was a beautiful evening and the sun had just set. We lined up in the street all colored somewhat orange reflecting the afterglow. "As I call your last name, answer with your first name and middle initial," shouted Captain Nobles. He completed the list of the whole company when Maniscelli came running out of the barracks and asked, "What's the drill?"

The captain explained patiently, "Reply with your first name and middle initial. Maniscelli!" "Peter P." shouted Maniscelli and the whole formation broke out in laughter. Normally it would not have been funny, but everyone was in such a good mood and pleasantly excited that it was.

"When I give you 'At ease' you will load up all your gear and prepare to move out. We are going down the hill to the railroad siding where we will board a train that will take us to a ferry at Weehawken, and the ferry will take us to our ship. I know those duffel bags are heavy and awkward, so each man in line help the man in front of him. At ease! Pick 'em up!"

We were like a bunch of old women at a department store sale as we bumped into each other trying to swing our duffel bag up on top of our pack and still hold our rifle slung over the right shoulder. The good humor suffered a bit as men shouted and swore until at last, somehow, we were all lined up ready to go.

"Company, 'Ten-hut! Right, face! Forward, route step, march!" And so began our journey to the big unknown. We did not have time to dwell on it as after a few steps we soon felt the edge of our steel helmets being pressed down our bare necks as the weight of the duffel bags perched precariously between the tops of our stuffed packs and our helmets. Also, the metal clip on the gas mask case that hung under the left arm began to dig into your side, and you did not dare reach over to adjust it as you might dump the whole load on the street.

We felt like a formation of turtles as we waddled down the hill to the tracks. Somehow we all made it down the hill and stumbled into each other as we arrived at the big green Pennsylvania Railroad cars with the red and gold emblem on the side. There was a collective sigh of relief as we got the OK to drop our bags on the ground.

We clambered up the high steps to get into the coaches and dragged our duffels along the aisle to a seat. We wedged ourselves, wearing our full field packs, two to a seat with our duffels in the aisle and our rifles in between. Fortunately, it did not seem to take too long to ride to Weehawken. Had it been any longer, they would have had to use crowbars to pry us apart.

Once more we had to hoist those bags up on our necks, and everyone was complaining about the weight of all those extra personal items we had stuffed into the B bags. Just then some of the headquarters platoon sergeants came along, and if you had a free hand showing, they gave you a box of company records to carry with you. I was given one and it weighed a ton!

We passed through the ferry terminal to get on the ferry, and they must have placed some barrier to keep the crowd of civilians back. Although we could not see them because our heads were bent down under the heavy load, we could hear them cheering and it made us feel better.

Now a new challenge arrived. We were herded onto the ferry and wedged together standing up with our full loads, and the ferry boat began to sway as we moved out of the pier and down the river. Soon we realized that we couldn't fall under that mass of humanity as we were packed in too tight. Some guy next to me in that darkness told me in unprintable language what he planned to do to me as soon as we got aboard because the upper corner of my pack kept hitting him in the eye. At this point, I didn't care.

After an eternity of swaying against other men in that black hole, we finally disembarked onto a pier at Staten Island. When we were able to drop our bags, we could finally look up and see our ship. The USS *Argentina*. It looked pretty big.

Once more we lined up and were checked off by name. Someone said General Paul was standing there but I never saw him. Some others must have seen him as they yelled "OK Gangplank, are we really going this time?"

Here we go. Up with the duffel bag once more and stagger toward the end of the pier. There was a Red Cross man standing by a table, and he had a small brown paper bag for each man. We had no more hands to take it, so he put the tops of the bags in our mouths.

We thought this was bad until we came to another man who had a red cardboard ticket. He said, "This is your meal ticket. Don't lose it or you won't get fed." And he jammed it into our mouths beside the small paper bag that contained a deck of cards, a pack of gum, a candy bar, and a missal. The man with the bag had asked us if we wanted a Catholic missal or a Protestant testament.

So this is how we go to war, I thought. In the movies the band would be playing as Randolph Scott or John Wayne proudly marched in sunshine, in dress uniform, onto the pier as his dad, in a blue suit and gray homburg hat, stood smiling next to the colonel and waving "Good luck, Son." Girls would be blowing kisses, and everyone would be smiling as if they were at a wedding reception.

"Move it soldier! Up the ramp!" Man, this doesn't even look like a gangplank where people walk up single file. This looked like a ramp where you drove cars onto a boat, and we went right into the side of the ship and then started to climb stairs. Bump! Crash! "Watch it! Hold it there!" More shouts. "Who's leading this mess?" "I don't know, but I hope he knows where he's going!"

Down endless passageways we went until at last we halted and could drop our duffel bags. I then had a free hand to remove from my mouth the paper bag I had been gagging on, also to remove the meal ticket. I was so afraid of losing it that in my anxiety I had bitten a hole clear through the cardboard. My teeth marks made a semicircular scar on the card.

Our platoon of thirty-four men was assigned a stateroom on B deck. What had been a stateroom for two people now held all of us. To accommodate all of these bodies and gear, they had built pipe frames from the deck to the ceiling. Each oblong frame was roughly three feet wide and six feet long. Wound around the metal pipe was a tent rope that fastened through eyelets on a piece of canvas to form a hammock. These were stacked about five high with a narrow aisle in between the stacks.

Into the narrow space between the stacks of pipe frames you had to squeeze your body, pack, rifle, and duffel bag. As you lay on your hammock, the space above your body was determined by the weight of the man above you as his hammock sagged down above your nose. As it happened, I had Frank Arrighi, a big man from Beverly Hills, California, above me and his avoir du pois severely limited my breathing space and lateral movement. The odor from all those sweaty bodies was definitely not something to write home about.

There was one porthole in our stateroom, which was open for air during the day but had to be closed at sunset every night to keep from showing light to enemy U-boats. The aisle space was so limited that we could not all stand up at one time. If we had been hit by a torpedo, it is doubtful we could all have gotten out of there.

There was a small bathroom with a shower, toilet, and sink. We soon found out that the water in our bath was salt water from the sea. One could not develop any lather from soap and did that razor pull across your face when you tried to shave.

For drinking water we had to use our canteens and refill them from faucets in the passageway marked "Safe drinking water."

It seemed to take all night to get everyone on board and into assigned locations. In the morning we slid out of our sacks to get ready for chow. We had to take turns in the latrine one at a time and then file out to the passageway. Our platoon sergeant led us down to the mess hall, which contained stand-up tables built in a row with pipes running up through each table to hang on to if the sea got rough.

We each took a tray and got our first meal aboard—powdered eggs, toast, and coffee. When the mess attendant punched out a hole in our meal tickets, I noticed that other men had teeth marks in theirs too.

After chow time we were permitted to go up on deck but were limited as to where we could go. With 10,000 troops aboard, it would be possible to capsize the ship if we all went to one side at the same time.

The sun came out as we got on deck and we could look out on Staten Island and other ships, in the harbor and at other piers. Guys were joking about taking a cruise to Europe and asking "How are your accommodations? Have you met the cruise director?" We thought we had it rough until we talked to the guys who were quartered in the hold. We all wondered where the officers were quartered. Typical GI humor and imagination came up with some wild suggestions.

As the ship eased out of the dock and turned to start down the river to the sea, I was eager to see all the ships in the harbor and to look up at the *Statue of Liberty,* which I had seen two years before on a trip to New York with my father. I was telling Vic Martin and Lambert Ciancaglini all about it when a voice came over the loudspeaker, "There will be a Sunday Mass for Catholics at ten o'clock in the mess hall. For a moment I considered missing Mass and staying on deck with the others to see the statue. Then my better sense took over, and I headed down the stairs to Mass. As soon as Mass ended, I hurried up the stairs and rushed out on deck to see water, nothing but water. Well, Old Girl, I will just have to wait for the return trip to see you again.

As we headed out to sea, ships began to collect around us in all directions. It turned out that we were the flagship of the largest convoy of ships to cross the Atlantic. We felt somewhat assured when we could see an aircraft carrier on the port side and one on the starboard side running parallel with our ship. We did not learn until we got across the pond that the ships were not operational carriers but were being used as transports.

The next day a cry went up from many GIs, "Look! Nurses!"

There began a battle to get to use a sergeant's field glasses to get a better look at the nurses who were on the carrier's deck playing with a big ball. Fortunately, there were nurses on the decks of both carriers or else the pell-mell rush to the rail and portholes on one side of the ship might have capsized the vessel. There would not have been enough MPs to hold back the excited GIs.

On board, the Army tried to maintain some form of discipline and set up a training schedule. Our company took its daily turn on deck to conduct calisthenics. Each of us had been issued a dark blue, stuffed life jacket with a battery-operated red light attached. It was comical to see us all try to jump and bend over wearing all this gear.

After a few days of getting our sea legs and getting used to the daily routine, boredom began to set in. That is when the Army Special Services came up with thousands of pocket books for us. They were paperback books that looked like full-sized books reduced to half size. Surprisingly they were not cheap pulp novels, but were really good stories, many of them classics.

You could see GIs everywhere reading these books. Stretched out in their hammocks or squatting on the upper decks, guys were immersed in the books. We had no radios or newspapers, so guys who never read a book in their lives were reading one now. Soon the great trade began, "I'll trade you *Treasure Island* for *Moby Dick*," or "I've got dibs on *All Quiet on the Western Front* as soon as you finish it."

Not everyone was an avid reader. There were groups of GIs who had regular spots on deck where they would assemble every afternoon to wager on the galloping dominoes. The dice games occupied all the deck space against the bulkhead, seemingly by Divine Right, and those who walked on deck had to walk over against the rail.

It was interesting to watch as the GIs sat in a semicircle facing the bulkhead. Each game had an "operator" who called the game. "Shooting seventy!" (Meaning seventy bucks. We still had our American money.) "Here's twenty!" "I've got ten!" Until someone shouted "You're faded!" And then the dice were thrown.

What always amazed me was how the operator knew who to give the money to when the player lost. Ten and twenty dollar bills were thrown onto the deck in a pile, and he would pass them out. Yet I never did hear anyone complain about not getting the right amount.

Las Vegas could not have more professionally run the game. The operator got a "drag" from the pot after a third "pass" or win. Seems to me it paid better to be the operator than a player. All of this is part of the education one receives as an infantryman.

In the early evening, right after supper, a guy would come on the loudspeaker and announce: "It is now sunset. All portholes will be closed and dogged down until sunrise tomorrow." He had the same voice as the guy who used to be the announcer for the movie travelogues, remember? "As the sun slowly sinks in the west we say goodbye to Pago Pago."

Each door leading out to a deck was sheltered by a three-sided wall to block any light from escaping. On deck all was darkness as we shuffled along. Woe to the man who decided to try out his little red light on his life jacket. The screams of nearby GIs were loud enough to be heard on the U-boats.

Ciangi and I used to hang over the rail and talk about what we would do after the war was over. His home was in Wilmington, Delaware, and he would describe every house and movie theater. My home was in Altoona, Pennsylvania, and I would tell him about my family of four brothers and three sisters. One night Ciangi got sort of solemn and said, "I wonder how many of us will be coming back?" In my youthful innocence I said, "We will all come back!" "Oh, no we won't" he said. Later events proved him to be right.

One evening I stood alone at the rail looking out at the blackness of the sea broken only by the whitecaps of the waves. I said to myself, "How did I get here?" and I started to look over the past year.

On May 18, 1943, I skipped school for the morning and went to the armory and enlisted in the Army. Since I was then only seventeen years old, they did not call me for active duty until after my eighteenth birthday on June 4th and my high school graduation of June 10th. So, on the morning of June 25th, I said goodbye to my family and several high school chums and boarded a train for New Cumberland Army Depot, an induction center at New Cumberland, Pennsylvania.

On the third day there, we went down the line inside a big long building dressed in our civilian clothes and came out the other end wearing a complete uniform and carrying a barracks bag full of clothes. We felt like real soldiers, and every day we waited to be shipped out to our training bases. Finally on the twelfth day we were loaded on a train for Spartanburg, South Carolina. When we stepped off the train at Camp Croft, I thought someone had left the oven door open. It was hot!

In the first few hours, we were assigned to the first platoon of C Company, 35th Infantry Battalion. Then we met our drill sergeant, Harry Schutt, who came from Mount Carmel, Pennsylvania.

Life really changed. We weren't soldiers, we were "meatheads." Most of us were fresh out of high school and rather sheltered home lives. It came as quite a shock to be constantly yelled at and treated as if we were really low life.

Sergeant Schutt and Corporal Mazanowski were northerners and at least we could understand them. The rest of the cadre were southern boys with a real drawl and I, at first, thought they were speaking a foreign language. It took awhile to catch on.

Every morning we arose at 5:00 A.M. and drilled all day in the hot sun. We learned to live with our M-1 rifle, to take it apart and clean it.

Our hikes kept increasing in distance. First five miles, then ten, fifteen, and finally thirty miles night hike with full pack.

The Army's purpose was to train us in weapons and to toughen up our bodies to be able later on to withstand the rigors of combat.

Lt. Joe Cadden was our platoon leader, and we all grew to have the greatest respect for him. While the sergeants all yelled at us, Lieutenant Cadden only encouraged us and talked about what a great platoon we were.

When we went on hikes, Lieutenant Cadden always went with us all the way. Other officers didn't always do this. I remember a Lieutenant Vibbeart who rode out on a truck and joined us at about mile twenty-five of a thirty mile hike and immediately let us know he was there by shouting, "All right! Pick it up! Hut, two, three, four. Hut, hut!"

Each man fought his own body. You wanted to drop out from sheer exhaustion, but you did not want to lose the respect of the other men. Inside they were feeling the same way about you.

I used to tell myself I could make it to the top of the hill and then I would drop out. When I got there, I said to myself I will go as far as that light, and so on, all night long.

We were building up our endurance, but we were also building up our group pride and our own personal confidence.

These were things we needed later in combat. At the time, we thought the Army was cruel and the sergeants vicious and vindictive. We did not realize that they were tough on us so that we would toughen up and be able to handle the stress of war.

We all wanted to kill our sergeant. I remember walking up the hill from the PX at Camp Croft talking to John Burak, my squad buddy from Wilkes-Barre, Pennsylvania. We both agreed that Sergeant Schutt would not last long if he ever went into combat with our platoon.

Our training was very realistic. We crawled under barbed wire as they fired machine guns with live ammo only thirty inches above us. If you panicked and stood up, you would be shot. There were holes we had to crawl around where dynamite was blown up to simulate mortar shells. If you crawled into a hole, you could have been killed.

After much time on the rifle range, I qualified as an expert rifleman and shot 98 out of 100 bullseyes at 200 yards. I received a medal for this and I wore it with great pride. I was the squad leader for the first squad.

Near the end of our thirteen-week training, we engaged in what was called Village Fighting. There was a mock-up village that we attacked by squads firing live .30 caliber bullets from our M-1 rifles. I was nearly shot by John Anderson of Butler, Pennsylvania, as he fired through the window of a hut when I was inside it. Whew! Realistic training, I thought.

During our training, there was one training officer and one enlisted man killed on the Village course. I remember the lieutenant saying, "We lost one officer and one enlisted man. The score is even. Let's keep it that way."

By the end of the summer, we had become a real fighting unit with a real esprit de corps. We hated to say goodbye to our platoon mates as we were broken up into small units to be sent off to various colleges for the Army Specialized Training Program (ASTP).

All of us were imbued with the pride and respect for the United States Army Infantry that had been planted in us by Lieutenant Joe Cadden. Each day he talked about how the infantry wins all wars. He was quite a man and one of the best that I met while in the Army.

In October, I went with a group of about twelve by train to Morgantown, West Virginia, to attend West Virginia University.

What a change! When we got off the train, we were met by a fat little corporal who calmly said, "O.K. Follow me," and he turned and walked up the hill through town. We were all shocked at this lax discipline. What kind of post is this anyhow? We had no weapons or battle gear, and even our barracks bags were moved by truck.

As we got to the top of the hill, we could see many of the university buildings and then turned into a fraternity house. We each got a big bed with blue blankets, not even US Army blankets. The corporal said, "I'll be here in the morning at 7:30 to take you to chow." What, 7:30? Not 5:00 A.M.? We must be in heaven! I ventured a question. "Is the uniform tomorrow fatigues and leggings?" The corporal looked hurt, "Leggings! Please! No, just your fatigues."

What would Sergeant Schutt say if he were here? We were actually disappointed. Here we had been trained to snap to on command and this place must be another Army. It didn't take us long to explore and soon locate the girls in Terrace Hall just across the street. The girls were duly impressed with our uniforms and we felt like big dealers.

The next day we were moved down the hill to a dormitory building, and while it was not as plush as the fraternity house, it was sure better than our unpainted wooden barracks at Camp Croft.

For the next three months, the Army tried to make an engineer out of me. It didn't work. I had studied the academic course in high school, had French, Latin, English and history but very little math. No trigonometry, no calculus, no physics. I was lost.

After two weeks of trying, I realized that my days at WVU were numbered so I decided to enjoy myself. I went to all the dances and football games and dated lots of coeds. The food was terrific! I even got to hitchhike home to Altoona, Pennsylvania, for Christmas 1943.

When I returned from the trip home, I was informed by Sergeant Summers, who was also from Altoona, that I was going to be sent to join with the 26th Infantry Division at Camp Campbell, Kentucky.

Oh! No! Back to the infantry! In this cold and snow? I had grown soft and had fallen in line with the loose discipline at the school. However, a few nights later, six of us met out in front of the dorm, said goodbye to our buddies from Camp Croft, and loaded on a $2^{1}/_{2}$-ton truck for a cold ride over the mountains to Grafton, West Virginia, and a train to Bowling Green, Kentucky. When we arrived the next night at post headquarters at Camp Campbell, some unnamed lieutenant came outside and joyfully announced, "Congratulations! You are here just in time for winter maneuvers in the hills of Tennessee!" Hot dog!

We stayed overnight at a Division Headquarters barracks. Next morning we met with an officer who wanted MP candidates. He did not choose me, so I was soon dropped off with my duffel bags at Headquarters Company, 3rd Battalion, 104th Infantry Regiment. Inside the office I met Corporal Paul "Jake" Lipps who was CQ (Charge of

Quarters) for the day. I was asking him about the YD (short for the Yankee Division) when Lieutenant Scott came in. "Here's a new man for our company, sir," Jake offered. "Well, he looks big enough to lift heavy bales of barbed wire, so put him in A & P (ammunition and pioneer) platoon," said Lieutenant Scott as he left the office. Something about the lieutenant's demeanor turned me off right away, and I did not want to be in his platoon. Maybe it was the mention of "heavy bales of barbed wire."

As I talked some more with Jake, I learned that he was from Bradford, Pennsylvania, and I told him I was from Altoona. I gave him my last cigar, which he seemed to appreciate very much. He told me that he was in the AT (Antitank) platoon and there were several other Pennsylvanians in it. I asked him how I could get assigned to the antitank. He said, "Here comes the First Sergeant now. I'll see what I can do for you."

When the door opened and First Sergeant Doug Beck came in, Jake said, "Here's a new man for our company, First Sergeant. I've been telling him about AT and he wants to be in our platoon. Is it O.K.?"

First Sergeant Beck looked me over and said, "Yeah, I guess so. Have him report to Sergeant Piquette." Jake never bothered to mention that Lieutenant Scott had said to put me in the A & P platoon.

Jake directed me to the AT barracks and told me to report to Sergeant Piquette. As I entered the barracks, I was amazed to see the steps covered with mud and inside the floor covered with dirt. After the scrubbed barracks of the summer at Camp Croft and the shiny waxed floors of the college dormitory, I was disappointed to see such a mess. I had never been in the real army in the winter time. So this was it!

I asked the nearest GI where I could find Sergeant Peck. The guy roared with laughter and said, "I'll get him for you." He came back with a Technical Sergeant and said laughing, "Here is Sergeant Peck!"

What I had done was to confuse First Sergeant Beck with Sergeant Piquette. I thought to myself, "Boy, I am screwing up on my first day in the new outfit." However, Sergeant Piquette chuckled, welcomed me, and made me feel at home. He led me down the aisle to meet Sgt. Vic Martin, who would be my squad leader as I was assigned to his first squad. He was from Latrobe, Pennsylvania.

All of the other platoon members were looking me over and sizing me up. One of the guys in the first squad, "Pop" Willis, seeing my serial number, 13146453, stenciled on the side of my barracks bags asked me if I had just returned from Guadalcanal. Since all of these men were draftees, their serial numbers all started with the number 3. Since I had volunteered, my number started with a 1. Pop and some of the guys thought my no. 1 meant I had been in the Army longer.

When I told him that no, I had not been to Guadalcanal, but had just come from ASTP at West Virginia University, I was then labeled the "college kid." As long as I was in the YD, I never did live it down that I was a "college kid," as if it was a disgrace. They never could seem to grasp that I had infantry basic training and then the Army sent me to college.

The very next day we headed out in the blowing snow and cold for a field problem. That night I told Sergeant Martin that I would stand guard all night rather than sleep on the cold ground. The squad thought this was great as they could sleep all night. I could hardly wait for dawn, but I kept awake and on my feet all night.

When we got back to Camp Campbell, Sergeant Beck told me that I had a ten-day furlough due since my record did not show any since I joined the Army. I was thrilled and left by train for home the same day.

When I got home and surprised my folks as I walked in the door, my mother looked worried and asked, "What does this mean?" Since my brother Bill had come home on a surprise leave just before he left for the South Pacific with the Americal Infantry Division, she naturally thought that I was heading overseas in the next week or so. It took me awhile to assure her that it was a normal furlough.

I was only home a day or so when I came down with the flu, probably as a result of going from the warm college dorm to the field exercise in the snow of the hills of Kentucky. Still sick in bed as my ten days expired, we called the Red Cross to get my furlough extended. They sent a representative to our home to check me out so I did get an extension.

In two days I got a telegram to report to Camp Forrest at Tullahoma, Tennessee. After two long days on a train, I was assigned to a temporary detail at Camp Forrest where I did KP everyday for a week until I got a truck for the field location of the YD near Lebanon, Tennessee.

When I rejoined the AT platoon, I was derided for being that soft college kid who caught the flu after one day in the field. The ribbing continued for days since I was wearing a Class A uniform and could not work on the 57 mm AT gun and other details until my barracks bags with my fatigues, helmet, and gear finally showed up.

All through February and March of 1944, the YD fought the wet rain, snow, and cold slush of the Tennessee hills. It was real combat without actual firing. Later, in Europe, we would learn how well prepared we were for living and fighting in such weather.

As we traveled through the small towns, villages, and farms we got to meet and talk with a lot of civilians. I shall never forget the warmth and genuine friendliness of the Tennessee mountain people. Even though we were tearing up their land, smashing down stone walls with tanks, and cutting down lots of trees, they understood that it was necessary to train the troops.

One night I was standing by our kitchen tent while Sergeant Arruda, a mess sergeant, was cleaning the gas ranges, with the only light coming from the flame of the range. I was talking to someone near the tent entrance and was not aware that Arruda decided to fill the range tank with gasoline while the range was lit. WHAMMO! When the first gas fumes from the tank hit the flames it exploded, and I was blown clear out of the tent. My clothes and my hands were on fire!

Some quick-acting GIs nearby rolled me on the ground to snuff out the flames. Somehow, Arruda was not even singed. I must have caught the full blast. My hands swelled up like boxing gloves, and I thought they would burst.

Someone directed me to the Battalion Aid Station tent. The medic there got out some tubes of ointment to place on my hands, but the heat and smoke in the tent caused my hands to hurt so much that I asked the medic to come outside, which he did.

After he covered my hands with ointment, he wrapped them up in bandages and went back inside the tent. I walked up and down a dirt road all night holding my hands up in the air, because it hurt more if I held them at my side. No one thought of giving me anything for pain or evacuating me to a hospital.

For the next few days, I walked around like a zombie. Guys had to help me to eat and visit the outdoor slit-trench latrine. Since I could not work, they assigned me as full time guard at the latrine. Major Donaldson came to the latrine and when he saw my bandages he asked, "My God, soldier! What happened to you?" When I explained, he asked if I didn't want to go to a hospital and I said no. "Want to stay with your outfit then, good man," said the major as he left. After that the kidding of the college kid seemed to lessen.

One night we were involved in a night crossing of the Cumberland River. In the confusion, one of the boats carrying men of B Company became overloaded too much on one side and capsized. The men, wearing full packs, helmets, rifles, bayonets, and canteens spilled into the dark waters of the Cumberland. Lt. John Dunski and nineteen men were drowned in the closing hours of the final field problem of the maneuvers.

The next day, all of our guys were talking about how to drop your gear if you got dumped into the water. Obermeyer was pontificating with his view that you should hold on to your bedroll, as it would float and hold you up like a life preserver. He was showing his bedroll to everyone and demonstrating how to hold it. We all noticed that he did not demonstrate in the water though. I thought to myself, "You try it Obey. Not me. Wet canvas is heavy and it sinks."

Marty Agnew, Lambert Ciancaglini, and I got an overnight pass to Nashville, and we all got the urge to taste apple pie. We went from restaurant to restaurant and could not find any place that had apple pie. It became an obsession with us that we must find a place with apple pie. Finally, on the thirteenth try, we found a store that sold individual-sized fried pies that were wrapped in heavy waxed paper. We bought a bag full of pies and headed for a theater.

The theater was crowded on Saturday night, and we got seats on the front row of the balcony. We had gotten into the show in the middle of the movie, which was a picture about some Army nurses on Corregidor and it was at a very sad part. The whole theater was deathly quiet as the three of us started to break open our fried apple pies. The crackling sound of the wax paper being torn drew mean glances from all the people around us. So we tried to tear the paper off slowly, which only made the agony worse for all the moviegoers. But we had to have our pies, so we did. When the lights of the theater came on after the end of the feature, we were being pointed out as, "those soldiers." Many times after that, we would laugh and talk about the night of the apple pies.

"Ciangi," Marty, and I became very close friends during the maneuvers. We would go to Mass in the field on Sundays, when our chaplain, Father Lee, would have us kneel with one knee inside our steel helmet as we knelt in the mud. Marty, often called "Googs" because of his heavy glasses, was the guy who wrote a letter home for me when my hands were wrapped up due to the burns.

One day, I was surprised to see trucks arriving and dumping out hundreds of soldiers who were all dressed in clean uniforms and shined shoes. When I got closer, I started to smile as I saw they were all wearing the blue and orange Aladdin Lamp shoulder patch of the ASTP.

These were all the rest of the guys who stayed in college when I was shipped out to the YD in December. I renewed acquaintances with the guys who came from West Virginia University. At least they missed most of the winter in Tennessee, but now the Army fully closed the ASTP program and dumped them all here in the YD. They looked on me as a seasoned veteran since I had enough mud on me to look the part.

At last, the maneuvers were over and the 26th Division left by convoy headed for Fort Jackson in Columbia, South Carolina. We were glad to leave the cold and wet of Tennessee, but I started to remember the chiggers and moist heat of South Carolina from the previous summer.

We were rolling along and had crossed into South Carolina when our truck broke down and stopped alongside a farm area near Greenville. It turned out that parts would have to be sent back from Fort Jackson to fix our truck, so our squad was left there and the convoy kept going.

We built a fire by the side of the road and slept by the truck. We did not have any food rations, so we were on our own. I walked down the road to a house, and two kind old ladies took me in for supper and invited me back for breakfast. Since I had no money to offer them, I chopped a pile of kindling wood from a pile of logs that was stacked near the barn. In the afternoon, a truck arrived to take us to Fort Jackson.

It took us several days to scrub the mud off our clothes, trucks, AT guns, and so forth. We were all pleased to have Sgt. Joe Sorrentino back in a real mess hall, and he turned out some great meals.

We settled down to more training in the hot Carolina sun. We were finishing up a thirty-mile night hike when Joe Lieb, from Pittsburgh, Pennsylvania, who was in line behind me, was complaining to everyone around about the loud noise my boots made. "Look at those canal boats! What size are those Courtney?" he yelled. When I told him they were 12 AAA everyone shouted, "No wonder!"

Later, back at the barracks, my platoon mates insisted that I go down to Service Company and have my feet measured to see if I had been fitted properly. So I did. The supply sergeant was shocked to find I only needed size $10^1/_2$B. When I came back to our barracks wearing the new size shoes, Joe Lieb cheered. At the mess hall, guys came over to see the new shoes and kid me about losing the oars to my canal boats.

We got regular passes to Columbia and ate seafood at the Ships Ahoy restaurant on the main street.

On Sunday afternoon, thousands of GIs on pass would stroll up and down the sidewalks of Market Street, just to pass the time. Many local people would drive downtown and angle park, then sit in their cars to watch the parade of soldiers moseying along the sidewalks.

One time, an older woman called me over to her car window and asked, "Say, why do soldiers come here every Sunday and just walk up and down? I think that is silly."

I answered, "We walk up and down because we have no place to go and nothing else to do. You have a car and a home to go to, yet you come here and sit and watch. Which one of us is sillier?" She snorted, and I went back to strolling.

Having heard about "goldbricks" so many times and how they made goofing off into a science, I decided one day to try it myself. Seeing an opportunity, when we were not counted in formation, I hotfooted it across the parade ground and into the PX (Post Exchange) where I ran into some other men from my own company who were also goofing off. Dominick "Chips" Gerardi, who was from Berwick, Pennsylvania, said to a group of us, "Listen guys. We can't stay here. The MPs will find us for sure. Let's head up to the Post Service Club." Outside, we all agreed, about seven of us.

As we got outside, Chips, who had more experience at this than the rest of us, said, "We can't just walk up the road or we'll be caught for sure. Better to form a squad and march up there." So we did. Chips marched at our side like a squad leader and called cadence, "Hut, Two, Tree, Four," whenever we passed any officers or company formations on the road.

Suddenly, there was a jeep bearing down on us, and it had a red metal sign on the bumper with two silver stars on it. A major general! The jeep screeched to a stop right in front of us, and Chips called "Squad, halt!"

The general hopped out of the jeep and gruffly asked, "Who are you men? What are you doing here?"

Chips rose nobly to the occasion, stood at attention, as we also did, snapped a salute and in a commanding voice shouted, "Acting Corporal Gerardi, Sir. Escorting a detail to clean the Service Club, Sir!"

The general seemed satisfied. "Carry on then." Chips saluted again and turned to us and shouted, "Squad. Forward, march!" And we continued on our way. As the general's jeep roared away guys all grinned and yelled, "Nice work, Gerardi!"

When we got to the Service Club, we all bought ice cream and gathered up all the comic books we could find on the tables and then went outside and got under the club building, which was built up on piers about four feet off the ground. We stayed there all day and really got bored stiff. About four o'clock, we formed a squad, single file column, and Chips led us back to our company area, where we ran into Pinky Piquette, our platoon sergeant. When he asked where we had been all day, we all complained loudly about being sent on clean-up detail to the Service Club.

We got a shower, changed into Class A uniform, and fell out in time for 5:00 P.M. retreat. It was then I made a mental note not ever to be a goldbrick again. It was too much work, and I felt so guilty.

One day, when I was on KP, Captain Nobles came to inspect and complained about the dirty-looking wooden signs that were mounted on the outside wall of the mess hall over each trash can; Grease, Bones, and so forth. I spoke up, "Sir. If you give me the go ahead, I will have new signs made that you will be proud of." "O.K. Courtney, you can do it tomorrow. Tell Sergeant Piquette I gave you the job."

The next day, I found a long board and a saw, and I cut the board into six equal-sized sign boards. Then I located the regimental sign shop and a GI named Fitzpatrick who was the sign painter. He said, "There is some white paint. You paint the boards white and when they are dry, I'll letter them."

"Fitz" was a man of good humor, and as we worked together, I came up with an idea. We had read recently where Mickey Rooney, the actor, had been drafted into the Army. So I got Fitz to paint a big paper sign, 3RD BATTALION WELCOMES MICKEY ROONEY!

We agreed that we would not say a word to anyone and just put the sign out on a table to dry, even turned it so it read upside down. As guys came into the shop during the day, it was interesting to watch their reaction as they noticed our sign and then hurried out of the shop.

By the time I got back to our company and nailed the signs in place over the cans, the whole company was buzzing with the news about Mickey Rooney. One guy even swore he saw Mickey as Major Hanford's jeep driver. It was funny to watch the rumor grow and take legs. I never told the guys that Fitz and I had started it.

When I showed the captain the new signs, he smiled and said they looked good. I said, "Good enough for a three-day pass to Charleston?" He grinned and said, "Yes. Come on down to the orderly room and I will write you one."

In the following weeks, strong rumors persisted that we would soon be shipping out. These rumors were confirmed by Major Donaldson, our battalion commander, when one day during a field problem, he proudly told us that we would shortly be on our way to fight, "the German Army, the greatest army in the world." I thought to myself, "Really, I thought we were the greatest army in the world."

Somehow the word got out that everyone in the YD would get a fourteen-day furlough before we left Fort Jackson. It got so strong that everyone believed it.

It turned out that we were all supposed to get ten-day furloughs, but the feeling was so strong about the fourteen days that the upper echelons thought it would ruin our morale, so they came up with an announcement that we would get ten days plus two days "travel time" each way. The old Atlantic Coast Line Railroad got a real workout as thousands of YDers headed north.

It was great to be back home with my family in Altoona, but this time Mother knew for sure that I was headed across to Europe. Brother Bill was now an Infantry captain and moving up in the Pacific. Brother John was home from the 691st Tank Destroyer Battalion in Texas. He was discharged after a vehicle accident and some botched surgery. It was hard to say goodbye as I boarded the PRR train back south.

A few days after I got back to Fort Jackson, I returned from KP one evening to learn that I had been promoted to private first class.

Some of the men brought their wives back with them and got them rooms in Columbia. When the word came out that tomorrow was the day for our departure and that no passes could be issued for that last night, the telephones were busy as the guys called their wives.

The buses arrived from town that evening full of wives who were met by their husbands as they got off the bus. They had no place to go for their last hours together, except to spread out on the parade ground. That night, after dark, guys came back from the PX saying it was like an obstacle course on the grass. Fortunately, it was a moonless night.

The next day, we donned our packs and marched across camp to the railroad siding. All of the girls from the PX stood outside crying and waving as we passed by.

We loaded on the railroad cars, and as the train slowly pulled out of camp, we passed a group of German POWs, and I yelled out the window, "We'll send you some of your relatives!" I then got chewed out by Lieutenant Magee, as we were told not to talk to anyone outside the train.

The cars we were in were converted into sleepers by the erection of rows of bunk beds to replace the coach seats. I laughed to myself as I remembered seeing an ad in *Life* magazine saying, "All troops travel by Pullman."

Sometime before dawn, we stopped in Richmond, Virginia, and some nice old ladies brought hot coffee and cookies to the door of our "Pullman." I think we only had bag lunches to eat on the train.

Later in the morning, as our train came through Philadelphia, what a welcome we received! People everywhere were waving from windows, cars, and streets.

One girl in pink pajamas jumped out of a first-floor window to the cheers of the troops. All the way through the suburbs, the people cheered. Someone must have passed the word as they saw our uniforms. It made us feel great. The whole country was behind us!

The train slowed to a crawl through the railroad yards and Wisely, a GI from our company, said his father worked in those yards. He yelled to a track worker to call his dad. Soon we could hear a voice on a loudspeaker, "Wisely! Get that troop train! Your son is on it!"

We all started yelling, "Wisely! Here he is!" And in a few minutes the train stopped. Wisely saw his Dad. "Hey! Pop! Over here!" And his father came across the rows of tracks to our car. We were all grinning as father and son met. We sort of got a lump in our throats as we thought about our own fathers. In a few short minutes, the train started to move again.

At the end of our ride, we saw a sign, Camp Shanks POE. Our port of embarkation, at last.

We had more days of training, getting shots, and records checked. I remember the day we were herded into a big GI theater and a major got up on stage. "All right men, here it is! And this is no bull! Where you are going you won't be needing any money, so I advise you to send all your pay home to your folks. Fill out the forms before you leave this room for payroll deduction." So most of us did.

It was rather sobering when we were instructed how to make out a Last Will and Testament. Since I owned nothing to leave, I did not bother. I figured my GI life insurance would go to my mother and dad as beneficiaries. Very serious thoughts.

The last night before we got on board our ship, we were given twelve-hour passes into New York City.

I had always wanted to go to the Stage Door Canteen, which we had seen in the movies. However, I decided to go to the Bronx to visit the family of Marty Agnew, my pal who was left behind at Fort Jackson. We were all fooling around wrestling on the company street, when Marty sprained his ankle and couldn't walk. We all went to say goodbye to him at the base hospital before we left.

The Agnews were glad to see me at 288 Oliver Street, and I relieved their minds about Marty. They had not heard from him and assumed he had gone overseas. Mr. Agnew led me to a corner drugstore where I could call home to my folks.

Dad took the collect call, and I told him I was on my way to a great adventure. He gave the phone to my mother (we did not have extension phones then) and she got choked up. I tried to cheer her up and told her the war would be over before I got over there. She said that was the same thing her cousin Charles Rowan had said before he left for France in WWI. We said goodbye, and I walked back to the Agnew apartment with Marty's dad. Then I took the subway downtown and met some of our platoon at the ferry boat to Weehawken. Pinky Piquette was already on the boat and saw us coming so he pulled his tie loose, twisted his cap sideways and sprawled out on a bench to make us think he was drunk. We were all in high spirits, and we stayed on the ferry and crossed back and forth several times just to see the spectacle of the lights of New York. We knew it might be for the last time. We carried on joking and laughing like a bunch of kids.

"Hey, Courtney! What are you doing? Were you asleep?" It was Ciancaglini and he brought me back from my dreaming as the USS *Argentina* plowed through the night.

The next day was bright and sunny. The sea was very calm. We could see ships all around us clear to the horizon. We learned later that we were in the largest convoy of ships ever to cross the Atlantic.

The convoy was protected from German submarines, called U-boats, by small destroyer escorts, called DEs. DEs were very fast ships. When a U-boat was picked up on sonar, the DEs would rush to that location and drop depth charges, huge barrels of explosives. Thanks to the quick work of the DEs, not a single ship was lost in our convoy to Europe.

At 10:00 A.M. the *Argentina's* whistle blew. Soon all the ships around us were blowing their whistles too. It must have been a prearranged signal, as the whole convoy turned left in unison. We were all excited but knew nothing. The rumor mill was not working.

That evening, just before dark, the DEs began to churn back and forth between the ships and then started to drop depth charges which exploded in huge geysers of spray. One DE turned and headed back toward our ship's bow and blinked a semaphore (a blinking communications light) toward us.

Later, it all quieted down and we saw the tall cliffs of England shining a dull bronze color from the dying rays of the setting sun.

As soon as I awoke next morning, I knew something was up as the ship's engines had stopped. When we opened the porthole, I could see land. It was Normandy. We were off Cherbourg. In the harbor, I could see all kinds of boats and ships. The funniest one of all was a little tub that looked almost round. It had a French tricolor flag on it and three Frenchmen wearing berets and bobbing up and down as they neared our ship. All I could think was, "Rub a dub dub, three men in a tub" as these three unsmiling Frenchmen greeted our arrival.

We were all excited. Most of us had never been out of the United States before, and here we were in Europe.

We started to assemble our packs, thinking we would soon be going over the side on those net ladders that we had trained on back at Camp Shanks. Then a voice came over the ship's loudspeaker, "All right men! Before we leave we have to scrub down this ship. Cleaning supplies will be issued in your area. Make ready for inspection!" "Holy cow!" I thought, "Are we in the Navy?"

2

Normandy Hedgerows
to
Bois de Boulogne

To MY SURPRISE, ALTHOUGH WE HAD PRACTICED it so many times at Camp Shanks, we did not go over the side of the ship and down the net ladders. Instead, we came out a side door in the ship and onto a pontoon pier that had been floated out in the harbor and attached to the side of the USS *Argentina*.

Carrying our full packs and duffle bags, we waddled across the pontoon and dropped down into a rectangular-looking boat called an LCVP (Landing Craft Vehicle-Personnel). Once we were loaded, the boat took off, but we could not see out because we were below the sides of the boat. All we could see was a young kid with a white sailor hat who was apparently steering. I thought to myself, "Is that kid really going to get us ashore?"

Bump! Crunch! We hit the beach, and then with a loud screech, the front of the boat dropped onto the beach like a door on a hinge.

"Move out! Everybody forward!," someone shouted as we stepped out onto French soil. Believe it or not we were in Europe, and it was September 7, 1944. We dragged our bags up on the beach and turned to look back, what a sight to behold! The harbor of Cherbourg was full of ships of all sizes, and they were being unloaded by "ducks" (DUKWs), $2^1/2$-ton trucks equipped with propellers that ran on water and then had wheels to drive up on the beach.

We lined up there for hours until our whole outfit got ashore. It was like watching a huge ant colony as the ducks raced ashore loaded with boxes. As soon as they got up on the beach, they were swarmed over by men who unloaded the boxes and piled them on the beach. Immediately, the duck would turn back to the water and race back to a ship for another load.

What we could see of the docks and cranes was a mass of steel junk caused by the explosive charges set by the Germans to destroy them before they left. As we kept watching the unloading process, we noticed a fleet of trucks came continuously to be loaded from the pile of boxes on the beach brought in by the ducks.

Also, there were barges that floated in with large wooden boxes that had been lowered onto them by ships' cranes. We were told that these huge boxes each contained a $2^1/2$-ton truck disassembled to save shipping space. I never saw one being opened, so I don't know for sure.

Some local GI troops brought us some K-rations to eat and told us that they heard we were special shock troops brought over to crack the Siegfried Line. We thought we must be "hot stuff" and started calling each other "shock trooper."

Captain Nobles appeared and got us into a company formation. He said we were going to be loaded on trucks and taken inland to an assembly area. He said our area was B-52 and we were to remember it if we got lost.

Soon the trucks arrived and we piled on. We moved out right through Cherbourg and, for the first time in our lives, saw the destruction of war.

We looked up at the remainder of homes and apartments that had been bombed and shelled. It looked like pictures we had seen only two weeks before in Life magazine, only this time, it was real. We all pointed out the third-floor bathtub sticking out in the air all by itself, supported only by the drain pipe since the two floors under it were all rubble in the cellar.

As we moved through the outskirts of Cherbourg, French people came out to the trucks and gave us apples. One man had several bottles of wine, and I hastily got out my canteen cup which he filled with white wine. I remember the happy grin on Lt. Walter Cody's face as the Frenchman filled his cup too.

We did not tarry long because it started to rain. We moved out into the hedgerow country and were sobered to read the ACHTUNG MINEN signs and the signs attached to the hedges reading MINES CLEARED TO THE HEDGES. I made a mental note not to go beyond the ditches if our truck stopped for a relief break.

We rode on into darkness, and the rain increased and got heavier. We had no headlights, only the "cat eyes," which were little greenish lights mounted on the front and rear of each vehicle. The driver had to strain to see the cat eyes ahead of him, and the rain made it almost impossible.

At one point, our truck was stopped at a crossroads and an MP asked where we were headed. Our driver said, "We don't know. We just follow the truck ahead of us." "Are you part of the 104th?" the MP asked and our driver said "Yeah, the 104th." Then the MP said, "Turn right here and catch up with your outfit."

After several miles of rain on a narrow muddy road, we stopped at an opening to a hedgerow, and the driver yelled to a guard standing in the rain, "Is this the area for the 104th?" The guard yelled "Yeah!" and our truck turned into the hedgerow and stopped at a row of pup tents.

There was a muffled conversation between our driver and some men near the pup tents. We were anxious to unload and get settled. That is when an officer appeared and told us this was the 104th Division, not the 104th Regiment.

Great! Here we are lost in Normandy, and we don't even know where the front is. Why didn't the driver, or the man in the seat next to the driver, say 104th Regiment or at least ask for area B-52? It was just a typical army SNAFU (Situation Normal All Fouled Up).

We unloaded, shouldered our bags, and began to walk down the road in the rain. No one seemed to know why the truck was sent back and why we had to walk. It seemed to be hours before we got to area B-52, and the rest of the company wondered where we had been.

It was dark, still raining, and the meadow ground marshy as we unpacked our gear, paired off, and assembled our pup tents. What a night! It reminded us of Tennessee maneuvers. We lay down finally on the wet ground and, since we were so exhausted, soon fell asleep, no doubt dreaming of the dry bunks back on our ship.

Happily, the rain stopped and the sun came out the next morning. The kitchen tent was up, and we got our first powdered egg, French toast, and coffee as we looked for a dry spot to sit down to eat our first Continental breakfast. Lafayette, the Yankee Division has arrived again!

The company was lined up in our "field" fenced in by hedgerows. We were told that it would take several days for our heavy equipment and guns to be unpacked and assembled. Meanwhile, to get us back in shape, we would take a series of hikes around Normandy.

As we marched along the dirt roads, we saw much evidence of the recent battle. Destroyed farmhouses, ruined churches, and towns which were just rows of gutted stone buildings. I particularly remember Montebourg. It was just a shell of a town with pieces of mortar and stones lying all about.

The French peasants were calmly going about the process of putting the stones back in place to rebuild the walls of their homes. They had no plumbing or electrical wiring to worry about, just the walls and roofs. They went about their work as if they had done this before and were used to it.

I wondered to myself how Americans would react if their homes were shattered and towns leveled. I hoped we would never have to find out.

On one of these daily hikes, when we took a ten-minute break, I sat on a log by the side of the road, and a little boy about five years old came up to say hello. I opened a C-ration can I had in my pocket to give him the three round pieces of hard candy. His eyes lit up as he said "Merci!" Since the crackers from the C-rations were so dry and my canteen was empty, I decided to try my high school French on the boy.

"S'il vous plait, donnez moi une tasse d'eau" (Could you please get me a cup of water), I said in a French accent that Sister Adrian would have been proud of back at Altoona Catholic High School.

"Un moment," he said and hurried off. In a few minutes, he returned with the empty C-ration can full of water. "Merci," I said, "Vous êtes un bon ami!" Then I drank the water, completely forgetting the instructions we had to drink only GI-issue water.

"On your feet! Move out!" the sergeant yelled, and I waved goodbye to my little friend as we tramped on down the road.

One night there was a commotion at our company CP (command post) tent. We learned through the grapevine the next morning that two of the officers got into an argument, which erupted into a fist fight. We did not hear which two, but we all looked for bruises or black eyes during the morning hike. When we stopped for a break I yelled to Sgt. Pinky Piquette. "Hey Pinky. It used to be bad enough that we privates had to erect the CP tent. Now I understand we have to erect a ring too!"

Pinky and all the GIs around laughed and Captain Crissos, who was standing there, broke out into a big grin.

Each company field, such as ours, had a guard posted on the road by the hedgerow break that led into it. One day, I was given the duty.

I stood there for hours, and it was boring, so I took out a pocket book left over from the boat. I got so absorbed in the book that I did not look up quick enough to see the command car that suddenly roared around the corner and whizzed by. Screech!! The brakes slammed on and it started to back up. Oh, no! It was Colonel Colley, the regimental commander, and I had not saluted.

When the car stopped in front of me I saluted and the colonel screamed, "Get me your company commander!"

"Yes, sir!" I replied as I ran back into our field. All of our officer's were away so I located T.Sgt. Jim Moorehead who hurried out and reported to the colonel.

"This man did not salute! I want him put on punishment at once!" shouted the red-faced colonel.

"Yes, sir!" replied Sergeant Moorehead as the colonel roared away in a cloud of dust.

Jim Moorehead turned to me and asked, "Why didn't you salute him, Bazooka?"

"I didn't see him," I replied.

"Wait here until I get someone to replace you, and then you can go and be latrine guard."

So, in a few minutes I found myself standing by the officer's slit-trench latrine. The "guard" had the duty to ensure that all excretions were covered up with dirt, so that flies would not be attracted. He must also make sure that the canvas wall erected around the trench remained in place, so that officers could not be observed and their dignity offended. Latrines for GIs were uncovered, since they apparently did not get so easily offended. Anyhow, I settled down to finish reading my book in peace.

In our field, we were cut off from the rest of the world except for supper time when they had a GI radio playing in the mess line out in the open. We listened to the BBC and the female announcer, with the cute accent, as she reported "British Double Summer Time!" We did not get much news about Americans though, only heard how the British troops were winning the war with "smashing victories" and "jolly good shows."

As the platoon "scrounger," and one who could speak some French, it was up to me to find some candles for our tents at night. I wangled some chunks of orange-brown GI soap from our kitchen and found some French boys who said they could get some "chandelles." When they came back I offered one cake of soap for two "chandelles," but the kids were shrewd and knew the value of their candles. We finally traded one for one. Later, back at the kitchen, Mess Sgt. Joe Sorrentino caught me raiding the soap box again, but he relented when I explained that it meant our guys could have some light in their pup tents.

We made sure to have all tent flaps closed before we lit the candles because a Luftwaffe plane flew over our area every night about 9:00 P.M. We called him "bed check Charlie."

It seemed to rain about every day now, and one evening we stood around singing and ran out of songs we could remember. Ciangi had a gleam of triumph on his face as he sang, "The clouds have passed and stars peep out from under in September, in the rain!!"

I had been feeling bad all day. My throat ached and my head was hot. Ciangi said I had better check in at the aid station to see what I had. So I took his advice.

The doctor there took my temperature, looked in my throat and then looked alarmed. "Your temp is 104 degrees! You have to go to a hospital right away!" Before I knew it, an ambulance pulled up and I was loaded on to a stretcher, while I protested that I did not feel that bad.

The ambulance roared away, and I was lying on the stretcher hanging from four cloth straps attached to the roof. The driver must have been used to rushing wounded men to the hospital, or else he was late for supper, as he bounded down over the bumpy Norman roads.

"Wow!" I thought. "Let me out and I'll walk. If I'm not sick now, I will be when I get to the hospital." Finally, old "Barney Oldfield" pulled through a gate, and I began to have a vision of a hospital with beds and clean white sheets and pretty nurses. SCREECH! We came to a stop, and I swung back and forth on the straps like a circus acrobat. The back door was opened, and I was hauled out.

"Where is the hospital?" I asked one of the medics carrying me.

"This is it," he replied as we entered a long tent with a grass floor. I was rolled onto a canvas cot and covered with a GI blanket and shelter half. There was a blue down pillow but no pillowcase. There went my dream!

My driver turned out to be a nice guy. He brought me a mess kit full of food and sat on the next cot and talked to me as I ate. He had come from England, and he told me stories about digging foxholes in England before the invasion and then a guy came and sprayed the dirt around the hole with green paint to camouflage it from the view of the Luftwaffe planes. I told him maybe those were just Irish troops using the national color, and he grinned and said, "You're not so sick."

I settled down and was soon sound asleep. Early the next morn-

ing, I felt the canvas shelter half being pulled off my head, as I had
rolled up in it. Oh my! I have died and gone to heaven! There, close
above my face was this beautiful, blue-eyed, red-haired nurse. "Good
morning!" she purred sweetly, and my heart started thumping. "And
how is Lieutenant Shafer today?"

"I am not Lieutenant Shafer, I'm Private Courtney" I said.

"Oh! You're not! Then this is not the officer's tent! I'm in the
wrong tent!" she exclaimed as she recovered my face with the shelter
half.

I was still wondering what happened when a few minutes later the
shelter half was pulled off my face and there was Ma Kettle, the enlisted men's nurse. Heaven will just have to wait awhile, I guess.

After several days, I was discharged from the field hospital and
given a ride back to my company area, this time by jeep. While in the
hospital, I had written a letter home explaining I was in a hospital, but
not wounded, only had pneumonia. About a month later, I got a
letter from my brother John saying, "I know you said you had pneumonia just not to worry Mother and Dad, but I can take it. I know
you were wounded in battle, so write and tell me what happened."
Sorry, John, no Purple Heart.

When I got back to my company, I asked where everyone was.
"Did they leave without me?" Only a few men were in the area. Then
they explained that anyone with a GI driver's license was taken to form
the Red Ball Express. This was an endless chain of trucks that hauled
ammo, food, and medical supplies from the Normandy beaches to the
front. Each truck had a red ball painted on the right side windshield,
and that meant they had the right-of-way over any other vehicle. They
rode continuously, day and night, to deliver supplies to General Patton's
Third Army.

Later, our YD men were relieved of this duty and they all came
back with wild stories of their escapades. Doug Beck told us about the
topless dancers he saw through a cafe window as he drove through
Chartres. We heard how chocolate bars were better than cash. I got a
kick out of their attempts at French pronunciations. Chartres became
"Char-tures," according to Charlie Campbell.

We were all still wearing canvas leggings, which had to be laced up
our leg from the ankle to the knee. We had heard about the newly
designed combat boots that would eliminate the leggings. The Red
Ball guys had seen them as they delivered truck loads to the front.
Captain Crissos heard us talking and told us there were boxes of them
sitting on Omaha Beach. If we wanted, we could go down there and

find a pair. He cautioned everyone about mines, which were still there in places. "I can wait for them," I told myself. "I do not plan to visit Omaha Beach as a tourist." But I was in a minority, as many guys headed for the beach.

Later that day, the tragic news filtered back. When the men got down to Omaha Beach, they were told to stay out of areas that were taped off because the German mines had not yet been cleared.

One GI decided he wanted to see inside a French house on the other side of the tape. As he approached the house, he stepped on a "Bouncing Betty." The mine exploded, and he was severely wounded. An officer and two medics nearby rushed to help him and were followed by ten other L Company men. One of these men set off another mine, which killed five men and seriously wounded five others. A mine-removal squad from the Engineers had to be called to remove the mines before the casualties could be evacuated.

That evening, we went to a memorial Mass for the dead said by our chaplain, Father Pro. I remember before he said the Mass, Father Pro said to us, "Men, you never know when you crawl out of your pup tent each morning whether you will live out the day or not. Best be ready. I know. When I went down to the beach to give our men the last rites I knelt down in the sand. After the blessing I happened to look down and there sticking up out of the sand between my knees were the three prongs of a live Bouncing Betty. It sure makes one think doesn't it?"

Finally, the day came when our trucks and guns arrived. We loaded all our gear on the trucks, hooked up our 57 mm antitank guns to our $1^1/_2$-ton trucks, and moved out in convoy. We did not realize that we were saying goodbye to Sgt. Joe Sorrentino and the kitchen crew whom we saw again only once or twice through the end of the war. Maybe Regiment and Battalion headquarters ate from the kitchen, but we only ate field rations.

As we passed through Norman towns, we saw more destruction, especially at Saint-Lô. It seemed as if those naked walls left standing were ready to fall on us at any minute. We felt safer after we got through the town.

All day long, we drove across France in a drizzling rain along muddy roads. Occasionally, we passed long lines of German prisoners heading to our rear. Just about dusk, we pulled into an area near Fontainbleau called Bois de Boulogne, a heavily wooded area not far from Paris. The rain had stopped, and it got downright cool. We were surprised that we were allowed to build fires, which we soon did. We had a beautiful square fire of small logs separated by small wooden pegs. We stood around and told stories about the different types of fires we had built. The ring of men around the fire always got tighter as the fire died down. Sure enough there would always be a GI who would yell, "Heads up! More firewood coming through!" The guys would always open the circle to let him in. Then he would drop a handful of small sticks on the fire and rub his hands to get warm. Everyone would gripe loudly, "Where is the firewood?" but the guy only grinned as he was now in the circle close to the fire. A professional goldbricker!

The next day, we assembled before we loaded on our trucks. Captain Nobles gave us our final talk. "Try to get by wearing only your field jacket. Always keep in mind that when it really gets cold, you'll have something left in reserve to put on. We are moving up to the front line tonight, so if you haven't cleaned your weapon today, by tonight you might wish you had. Good Luck!"

3

Alsace-Lorraine and the Siegfried Line

ON OCTOBER 6TH, WE MOVED PAST NANCY and assembled in an area around Arracourt. We were about to relieve the 4th Armored Division, which had halted its advance. There was an eerie fog late that afternoon when Sergeant Piquette took Jake Lipps, Robbie Robinson, and me in a jeep, driven by Art Poulson, up to our forward positions.

All around us on the hilly landscape were wrecked German tanks, mortars, dead horses, and cattle and a weird atmosphere of rising fog that made it seem like the landscape of the moon. Pinky turned in the front seat and kept looking at me as if he thought I would crack up at any moment. In his mind, I was still the college kid who made a joke out of everything.

"Don't worry about me Pinky," I thought. "I am O.K. I am not about to crack. This is a new experience for me and I am just taking it all in."

The jeep stopped behind a clump of trees, and we got out. Pinky led us forward to three spots where the 57 mm antitank guns were to be when they came up that night under cover of darkness. Robbie, Jake, and I were from three different squads, and we each began to dig our foxholes at our squad's gun locations as Pinky and Art headed back.

As it got darker, it began to rain. We did not know how far we were from the German lines, only the general direction. We did not see anyone on either side of us, and we kept digging.

Sometime about midnight, the three of us gathered together in the rain to talk about our situation. We agreed that the antitank guns were probably not coming up tonight. Since we were not sure where we were compared to German troops, we thought we might wind up in a very exposed position in the morning, so we agreed to try to find our way back to our lines.

About this time, we could see a man approaching from our left flank. As he got closer we yelled, "Halt!" He identified himself as being from K Company and said he was supposed to get coffee somewhere, so we let him pass. We then realized that no one had thought to give us the password and countersign for the night. First night in combat, SNAFU, I guess.

We headed back in the direction we thought was our rear, after an argument as to where each of us thought it was. I was outvoted, so we went where Jake and Robbie thought our rear was. It turned out I was wrong, and they were right. It reminded me of a similar situation I faced one night in South Carolina during basic training. I was wrong then, too.

Ater sloshing through the rain and fog for several hundred yards, wondering how we would get admitted to our lines without the password, a voice called "Halt!" Then he coughed. I recognized his cough. I yelled "Windell!"

He yelled, "Yeah."

I yelled, "It's Dick Courtney!"

He replied, "Come on in Courtney!" And so we did. Whew! Once again, it proved an advantage to know your fellow comrades—their voices, coughs, footfalls. In the YD we had trained so long together that we were well acquainted as a unit. We lost this edge after a lot of·casualties in Alsace-Lorraine and later in the Bulge.

We were led by Lewis Windell down a gully to Battalion CP, which was in a former German pillbox. The battalion commander, Major Donaldson, was in a bedroll on the floor. He woke up and asked the duty sergeant if Sergeant Piquette had moved up with his guns yet.

The sergeant said, "No, here are the three men who were out there on the gun positions."

"Wake me up the minute that the guns come up," said the major, as he turned over in the bedroll.

The next morning, we learned that our platoon leader, Lieutenant Matthews, decided not to bring the guns up in the rain and darkness. He was relieved of command, and we never saw him again. We heard rumors that he was assigned to a line company and sent out on patrol.

He was British, and his father lived in London. I remember that he shared a bottle of Scotch with our platoon the day before. Later, we learned the password was Custer and the countersign was Big Horn.

The next morning, we moved our three guns up in front of the ruined village of Rechicourt-la-Petite.

We dug in on a reverse slope with the idea, as Sergeant McKittrick told us, that we would shoot the tanks in their underbelly as they came over the ridge. In the fields around us lay dead Germans and dead cattle and smashed equipment. After I dug my foxhole, I made a roof for it of empty wooden German shell cases, then piled dirt on top of them. My hands were gooey with mud from this, so I washed them in a nearby stream.

The next day, J. A. Martin and I went out on our right flank to check on what appeared to be a squad of Germans out in a meadow. We approached with caution and our weapons ready, only to discover they were all dead.

These were the first dead Germans that we had seen up close. J. A. and I looked them over to see their equipment and weapons. There were six men, all with blackened faces, who were apparently on night patrol and were caught by mortar or artillery fire when they had no cover or chance to dig in.

The war seemed real now as we looked into their faces. They were all about eighteen years old and sprawled just as they fell. Most of them were on their backs.

One thing I noticed was the inscription on their belt buckles It read, *"Gott mit uns,"* which means "God with us." This was a real surprise to me as we heard how Hitler had decreed there was no God; yet, here were German army-issue belt buckles reading *"Gott mit uns."*

I don't remember ever looking closely at any SS soldiers' belt buckles. I'll bet they did not have any reference to God on them.

When J. A. and I got back to our squad area, we found that some of the guys had used their trench knives to cut into a few dead French cows lying about and were cooking steaks over a small sterno stove. I had qualms about how long the cows had been dead and whether they were diseased or not.

Someone said, "Don't worry. The Army gave you so many tetanus shots that you are immune."

The steaks looked better than C-rations, so we ate them.

A lieutenant from M Company came by and I offered him and his men some steaks.

He said, "No thanks. C-rations are enough for us."

I thought to myself, "He is right and probably more disciplined than we are." We never did cut into any more dead cows again. However, no one had any stomach or bowel problems after eating our French meal.

The Krauts soon sensed that there was a new outfit in place and decided to say hello to us with a mortar and artillery barrage. We had parked the truck in a ditch by the stream, and I was on top of the truck unloading ammo when the barrage started. I made a beeline for my hole and dove in. I was glad I had made a roof. Right behind us Pop Willis got some shrapnel in his leg from one of the shells.

The next day was Sunday, and since there was no way of getting to Mass, I took out of my shirt pocket the little Missal that the Red Cross man gave me back on the Staten Island pier. Although I was raised Catholic from birth and went to Mass every Sunday, the words of the Mass in that little Missal stood out from the page as never before. It hit me then! This is for real! "This is My Body! This is My Blood!"

I was just past my nineteenth birthday when, deep down, I really committed myself to Jesus Christ. It has remained the same with me for over fifty years. From that moment on, I really did turn myself over to the Lord, and he has always taken care of me.

Somewhere, I read one of Ernie Pyle's columns in which he tried to explain the mental process each man goes through as he approaches combat. Now, looking back, I can say that I was never really afraid to the point of panic or paralysis. Somehow, based on my faith in God, I believed that I would never be hit. Other guys would be, but not me. I did not think that I was better than other guys, but I had supreme confidence that with all the people at home praying for me that I would come out O.K. I think it was this attitude that carried me through the war when other guys cracked up. Some shot themselves in the foot, and so forth. I am still grateful to the Lord for protecting me.

Pinky Piquette, many years after the war, told my wife that he could never get me to take the war seriously. I did take it seriously, but I did not worry about it, and I tried to keep good humor going wherever I could.

After a few days of artillery fire, we did lose Sergeant Obermeyer. He was not hit by shrapnel, but his loud, raucous, commanding voice became a whimper. The guy who was mister muscles and was built like Hercules folded when the crunch came. Even before we got into a firefight, Obey claimed he was sick in his stomach and wanted to be evacuated. They tried to talk him into toughing it out, but he insisted he wanted to go back. The day he was supposed to leave, I talked to him. He said, "What do you think Dick? What will the guys say if I go back? Will they call me yellow? I'm sick, that's all. What do you think?"

"I think you should go back Obey, no matter what they say. You aren't going to be any good up here, and it will get worse than this. Go ahead and go back."

Obermeyer left, and we never heard about him again. Once in awhile, someone would wonder out loud what Obey was telling the guys in the rear echelons about his days at the front. They wondered if he got his big, loud, bombastic voice back. It was better for him to go back. As a squad leader, he might have held back in an attack or retreated from a position and jeopardized the lives of the rest of us.

It was mid-October and the weather was somewhat warm but with regular rain that turned everything to mud. Now we know what they mean by French mud. It is the stickiest glue in the world, and we all said we would package it after the war and sell it.

We were all apprehensive as to how we would do in actual combat. My one fear was that I would run out of ammunition. I had mental plans to keep a box full of loaded clips of ammo for my .30 caliber carbine on the truck. I visualized myself firing continuously.

The Germans had two strong points extending into our lines, and the 3rd Battalion was given the mission to straighten out the line and secure better observation points on high ground. We soon learned that the Krauts were experts at seizing and holding the high ground everywhere.

K Company led the attack through Moncourt Woods, and we moved up behind them to support. Here we hit our first machine gun fire and some artillery. K Company lost three men but cleared the woods and took some prisoners.

The Germans held higher ground near Bezange-la-Grande and were looking down our throats. Our advance was held up here until that hill could be flanked or neutralized. Our squad was on the edge of the woods looking out over a short valley in front of us. We dug our gun in and then dug our foxholes inside the woods. Since we were there for about five days, I really improved my hole, covered it with logs and dirt, and made it L-shaped for extra protection. I even placed two wooden boards into the dirt walls and mounted small candle stubs on each so I could read after dark. The rest of the squad called it Courtney's pillbox.

I had to leave the comfort of my pillbox as we moved up to support I and K companies' attacks near Moyenvic. We spent a wet, cold, miserable night on the side of a hill. I got into a barn and buried myself in a thick pile of hay, as I was soaked to the skin. In the morning, I awoke to drier clothes thanks to the warmth of the hay. I also had a terrible earache. I thought I had wedged a tassel of wheat into my ear. After a few days the pain went away. Right before the attack on the high ground to our front, we heard the roar of planes and prepared to duck for cover when we discovered they were American P-47s. Wave after wave they came in and strafed and bombed the German lines. We got out of our holes and watched as if we were at the Cleveland Air Races. Guys were yelling, "Give it to them!" and "How do you like it now, Krauts?"

After the airplanes finished their job, we all moved forward and through the woods and hills. At Vic-sur-Seille, we were held up at the river by a blown bridge. The Engineers came forward and slung a Bailey bridge across the piers of the blown bridge. This was done under fire and took real courage to complete. We were all glad to have the Engineers.

After we raced across the Bailey bridge, we ran through an open barn and out into an orchard. The man right ahead of me was hit and fell dead face down on top of his bazooka.

Other men from I Company ran through the orchard and lined up, about ten yards apart, along a stone wall. Although we were always taught in training never to look over a wall as the round steel helmet makes a good target, several men did and were shot through the head by snipers. I decided to look between the cracks of the drywall. We moved on across the field and continued our attack.

After we dug in for the night, we began to realize that in combat some men must die. Seeing guys you know lying face down on the ground makes you realize this, but you have to move on.

We got into Hampont at night, and the whole town was on fire. I remember Henry Jackson saying, "We'll remember this the rest of our lives." Little did we dream how often this scene would be repeated in the future.

I carried a bundle of straw for a long way from a barn to my newly dug foxhole, when we got orders to move again. Our two squads moved into Sotzeling. The Germans held the other end of town.

That night we were in a stone house where a French girl named Maria made some hot milk for Frank Chapo, who had a bad cold. He thought hot milk would cure his cold like his mother told him it would. Maria laughed at the word "French" for *"Français."* She kept calling her mother "French."

In the morning, the Germans started to move out. Vic Martin's squad was moving their gun to shoot a tank on the hill, when a TD (Tank Destroyer), just arriving, fired and destroyed the tank. One of the other Tiger tanks fired a shell, which hit the building we were in, and Cpl. Joe Masana took the full blast of white mortar in his face. Medics took him back later.

We picked up a good number of prisoners here, and they were quite scared. They had been told that the Amis (short for Americans) shot all prisoners.

We moved on to take Zeibling, and in the morning, the rain turned to snow. We could not believe it. The real white stuff! And now the winter to contend with! Hot dog!

We dug in on the side of a hill, and there were tanks and TDs parked in the field all around us. As we stood in the cold trying to keep our feet warm by pounding them together, I remarked how lucky the tankers were. "Look at those guys! They ride in an armored car. They stay nice and dry and they always have ten in one rations with them to eat."

Just then, a few mortar shells dropped on us, and the tank nearest to where we stood had the top hatch open. One shell dropped right through the hatch, exploded inside the tank, and killed five tankers. I didn't envy the tankers so much after that.

Robbie Robinson and I decided to go into a house to heat our rations on the Frenchman's stove. As we sat there eating our cans of meat and beans, we talked about what we would do after the war. Robbie said when he got home and got married, he would insist on his wife making baking powder biscuits every morning for breakfast. "Yeah!" I said, "and with peach jam too." "Of course with peach jam," said Robbie, with the assurance that all GIs had about their future dreams.

We were in the area of Conthil when K, L, and M Companies moved far ahead into Rodalbe without any armor support. Our whole battalion had moved so fast that our flanks were exposed and we were stuck forward in a very dangerous position.

We learned that we were fighting the German 11th Panzer Division, and they were veteran troops who had fought in Normandy. The Krauts soon realized the advantage they had and pressed into Rodalbe from both sides and encircled the town.

With tanks and overwhelming numbers of infantry, the Germans forced our troops to find cover in cellars. German sympathizers came out of their houses and directed the Nazi troops to the cellars where the Americans were hiding. The Tiger tanks would then depress their gun muzzles down the cellar door steps and fire 88 mm shells point-blank at the Americans inside. I Company tried to come up the road from Conthil but was driven back with heavy shell fire. The 4th Armored Division, which was our tank support, was held up by muddy fields and could not get to Rodalbe.

It was a bitter cold night in November, of freezing rain and snow, when Captain O'Neill, K Company CO (Commanding officer) and about sixty men broke out of Rodalbe and fought their way back to Conthil.

Another unit from Company G tried to break through to Rodalbe, but were all but wiped out. We were in a tight spot. The whole 3rd Battalion was almost wiped out. Heavy casualties were reported from the battalions on our right and left flanks. We all dug in to hold the high ground to keep the Germans from expanding their counterattack.

In the next few days, replacements were hurried in from the rear to fill in the ranks and once more, with armor support this time, we attacked Rodalbe. Once we got there, we found survivors from K and L companies who had hidden under piles of potatoes for three days with no food or water, except the spuds. Even K-rations tasted good to them.

One of the reasons that the civilians helped the Germans locate the hiding Americans is that Alsace-Lorraine was German from 1870 until 1918, when it became French again. The people there still had mixed loyalties. I could see it in their eyes every time we had to fall back from a German attack.

We moved into Château-Monfre to get reequipped and to receive replacements. We got four in our squad. We were eager to learn from them what was happening back in the States since they had recently come over. They said the people in the U.S. thought the war in Europe would soon be over. Wow! Maybe they knew something we didn't know.

I remember as we came down the main street in Bénestroff, which had been our division objective when we started our attack, Art Schwartz said, "Now this really looks like a German town."

I said, "What do you mean Art? This is still France." He showed me the style of the houses and why he thought they looked so German.

As Art pointed out, the style of the roofs was different from the French, and the windows were bigger and set back in big frames. Many windows had wooden flower boxes but, of course, no flowers in November. The town looked much cleaner, as many of the houses were whitewashed.

In one of the houses, we found some bottles of American whiskey. We did not know how they got there, but we left the empty bottles when we departed. Frank Chapo thought the whiskey helped his cold.

Near Val-les-Bénestroff we had to dig in because the bridge was blown. Sam Harper, one of our new men, and I dug in what seemed like solid rock. The next morning, as we moved out, an American tank came across the field right behind us and blew up right near the foxhole we had just left. We had slept in a minefield and didn't even know it!

We climbed a long ridge and arrived in Montdidier, the highest ridge in the whole area. Since our front was pinched off, we went into reserve for ten days. They brought up a projector and showed a movie in a barn. It was Kay Kaiser and his band, and we were thrilled. It was in black and white, and the projectionist said he had another movie that was in color and featured Betty Grable. All the GIs screamed to change the movie, so he did.

Several French peasant farm girls were raking up hay to feed their horses in the same barn, and when they saw Betty Grable and the other dancers in red tights and bare legs, they giggled with embarrassment. They let the GIs know that they thought we were not gentlemen to be watching such a movie. This was Montdidier, not Paris.

French farm girls were strong women. In this village there was a woman who was obviously very pregnant and that night about 11:00 P.M. the medics went to help deliver her new baby. The next morning, I was passing the barn and there was the new mother pitching hay up on the pile the same as she had done the day before. Strong women!

Thanksgiving Day came while we were here, and we were all promised a turkey dinner from our own company kitchen, wherever it was. All day we waited and finally, about 10:00 P.M. Joe Lieb drove up to our squad location in his jeep. "Here is your turkey guys, such as it is," he said.

We each got a big slice of bread which was wet and a big slice of cold, greasy turkey on top of the bread. Happy Thanksgiving! It was something different from K-rations, so we ate it. I did have qualms about the grease.

Soon after, I developed the "screaming GIs" and had to run outside in the snow. All night I ran outside, and each time soiled the white blanket of snow. The two GIs on guard laughed each time I ran out. "Here he comes again!" they would say.

The next day I was so weak and tired I went down to the other end of the village where the aid station was. I told T.Sgt. Steve Falkowski my problem. He said, "O.K. kid, this will fix you up. Here's a blue 88 (a GI name for a sleeping pill) and a cup of paregoric. Tell your sergeant to let you off guard duty tonight and take the blue 88, which will make you sleep, and the paregoric, which will tighten up your bowels." "O.K. Thanks, Steve," I said and headed back.

That night I took the pill and drank the paregoric. Now what happened? The blue 88 worked, but the paregoric didn't. I woke up soaked from my belt to the top of my shoes. The smell was somewhat neutralized by the smell of pigs in the next stall.

Now we did not have access to water, much less a shower, or a change of clothes. I stripped down and tried to scrape off my body with handfuls of straw from the stalls we were sleeping in. The guys in the squad were yelling, "Go roll it off in the snow!" Ha! I wrung out my long johns, shirt, and pants and put them back on just in time to move out for the next attack on Albertsdorf.

It was cold and snowing but no one wanted to dig in a foxhole with me. They never told us about this in basic training. Steve Falkowski roared laughing when I finally saw him again several weeks later.

It was weeks before our company was taken to the showers—which was not a warm, tiled bathroom with hot water and soap. We were piled on to open $2^1/_2$-ton trucks, driven for miles through the snow and wind, until we arrived at a long tent. At one end of the tent we were told to strip naked and to place our long johns, shirt, and pants on separate piles to be sent to the laundry. Then we ran through the tent through lukewarm water sprayed from an overhead pipe. At the other end of the tent, outside, was a pile of GI towels. You grabbed one and dried yourself in the cold wind. Then you began to hunt through the various piles of long john shirts, pants, OD shirts, and pants for your size. The short guys had no trouble finding small sizes. The rest of us yelled that these must have been brought from an outfit full of midgets! I needed a size 32 x 35 pants and when I could not find any, I was still naked in the snow and wind. I had to run around the outside of the tent back to the dirty piles and try to find my old pair and put them back on. Especially the pants, which had to be long enough to fit inside your leggings or your legs would freeze.

Back on the truck we griped all the way back to the front about the so-called showers. GI humor always arose to the occasion as someone yelled, "Wouldn't this make a great recruiting poster back home?"

A day later found us joining elements of the 101st Regiment in the attack on Sarr-Union, a city of some size. We climbed along a railroad embankment as the .30 caliber machine guns kept the Krauts, heads down. I remember that many of the windows of the hospital were shot out, as someone learned that the Germans were directing fire from there.

Our squad somehow got in to the town square ahead of the rifle companies, and we set up our 57 mm antitank gun on the cobblestoned street with the gun trails against the curb. We stayed down in the cellar behind the gun. The Krauts came back in counterattacks twice.

Once, I went across the street and through houses to try to shoot the German tanks from the side with my bazooka. I was all set to get one, when a TD blasted him in a shot from the town square. Great to have the TDs along. When I got back across the square to my squad, I learned that the Germans were in those houses on the side of the street where I had been.

Our regimental antitank company came into town to support us and set up on the other side of town. The next night, the Germans attacked in force and knocked out all five AT guns and their crews.

Sarre-Union was a tough town to hold onto. Maybe the Germans realized how much booze they left behind, because this was the home of the Pomeroi champagne distillery, which American GIs soon discovered.

We were there for several days, and we brought cases of cognac and champagne to our cellar. When we were on guard duty at night, we would lay on the outside cellar steps behind the gun and drink from magnum-size bottles of champagne. The Germans were on the other side of the street, but we didn't offer to share with them.

One day, Larry Choiniere, from Utica, Michigan, and I went through the apartments upstairs and brought down all the thick, silk-covered comforters from the beds and lined them across our cellar about four deep. It was quite a sight. We had pink, yellow, lavender, blue. We walked on them, muddy shoes and all. We wondered how the civilians would feel when they found all their bedding at one neighbor's house.

One morning Lieutenant Deviese came down the steps to our cellar, and we were lying on the quilts drinking champagne. I yelled, "How about this, Lieutenant?" and he smiled and said, "That's the changing fortunes of a soldier's life."

We found a warehouse full of cognac in dark green bottles with red seals on top. The older men used to explain to us kids about the three stars of Hennessey bottles and how that denoted top quality.

I used to say that the Germans could have won the war if they had poisoned all the booze, because GIs drank anything in sight. No one questioned the quality, and we all wanted cold and flu prevention for the winter. I guess maybe it is the same in all armies.

There was a general store in the southeast corner of the town square. Ted Holt and I decided to see if there was any food in there, so we entered and found another GI from I Company who had the same idea.

We found a few boxes, which I identified in French as something edible, so we started for the door. The man from I Company went out the door in front of me when a shell hit on the cobblestone street right in front of us. They say you can't see a shell explode but I did.

I saw a flash of light and little black pieces of metal rush toward us. The I Company man took the full blast in his chest and stomach. I was screened by his body and was not hit.

Ted and I dragged him inside the store and used Ted's emergency first aid pack as the I Company man's pack was smashed. We were trying to stop the flow of blood when a medic arrived and took over. The medic gave Ted a replacement first aid pack, since no man wants to be without one in combat.

Each man was equipped with a canvas-covered aid pack that fastened onto the front of the cartridge belt so that if you got hit, you could readily get out your aid kit. Inside the canvas was a small metal box about three by five inches and about two inches thick. There was a soft metal strap that went all around the can at the seam. When you peeled off this strip, the can opened into two parts. Inside was a gauze bandage and a container of sulfa powder to disinfect a wound.

You were supposed to sprinkle the powder on the wound to kill off germs, but I saw guys who tried to eat the sulfa powder. Either they were not well trained or they forgot because of shock.

Later, we learned that the I Company man died. We never knew his name.

As we left Sarr-Union, it was raining and the mud was so bad that we had to pull out the winch line from our truck and hook it around a big tree and winch our way up to the tree. Unhook the line and pull it out to the next tree, and so on, all the way across the muddy hill to Ormingen.

At the town of Kalhausen, we stopped long enough to get issued the long-promised combat boots. We were glad to throw away our old boots and canvas leggings and to strap on the new one-piece boots that covered our calves. Some wit suggested that the rear-echelon guys were all supplied with combat boots, so we could have them now. We all heard stories about the people along the supply line taking their cut and very little getting to the front-line troops. I remember Bill Mauldin, the cartoonist for *Stars and Stripes* (the GI newspaper), did a cartoon showing a big funnel of supplies, and Willie and Joe, the two GIs, getting a little drip from the end of the funnel. Mauldin's cartoons were always funny because they were always true to life at the front.

We came to Germany at last, a place called Achen. There were lines of "dragon teeth," as they were called. Row upon row of big cement blocks to form a barrier for tanks. They must have taken a long time to construct. It looked like an endless white cement fence that stretched for miles and out of sight. They were formidable, but our armor blasted holes through them, and we fought our way through the famous Siegfried Line.

I don't think anybody remembered the day we landed at Cherbourg, and the GIs there told us they heard we were special shock troops to crack the Siegfried Line. Well, here we were, in Deutschland.

When we halted our advance, we were surprised to see new troops arriving who all wore the yellow acorn patch on their left shoulders. It was the 87th Infantry Division that was left behind at Fort Jackson, South Carolina. They had come to relieve us. We looked hard to see if Marty Agnew was with them, but we never did see him. He was transferred to the 87th while he was in the hospital during our departure for Camp Shanks.

Ted Holt shouted, "Hey, Courtney, let's congratulate each other. We made it through the first sixty days!" We shook hands all around. It was great to be alive.

The next day we hooked up our 57 mm guns to the trucks and headed back to Metz for a rest. It was drizzling rain and the roads were muddy, as usual, but we didn't care as we were heading to the rear.

We had a heavy camouflage net that was supposed to hang over the gun to conceal us from planes, but we hardly ever used it as it was always wet, heavy, and awkward to set up. We also started out with two big, heavy steel plates about four feet square that were supposed to mount on hooks on the gun trails to protect us from small arms fire. The first time we saw armor-piercing bullets go right through these steel plate shields we managed to "lose" them during one of our moves.

Now, as we looked out on the messy, wet camouflage net which was perched on top of the gun, we saw our chance to "lose" it too. As we bounced along, the net began to slip off the gun and drag along the road. Our whole squad was cheering for it to go. Finally, only one snag held it to the gun.

"I'll get it!" Ted yelled and he crawled along the gun trails as the truck was still moving in convoy. He got to the gun and just as he reached for his trench knife to cut the net loose, he slipped and fell off the gun and was caught under the gun. We screamed to McGregor to stop the truck, and we rescued Ted from under the gun. He said good-bye as the medics took him away. Too bad we had to lose Ted to lose the net. I did get to see Ted in Paris after the war was over.

As our caravan reached the city of Metz, France, our division CG (Commanding General), General Paul, was standing there on the street to salute us as we passed. It felt very good. We were proud of our old YD, the Yankee Division, and we were proud that we had liberated part of France.

4

Battle of the Bulge

THE 26TH DIVISION HAD BEEN DEPLOYED to Metz for a rest after weeks of bitter fighting. We heard rumors there might be a Christmas party as we moved into a former French Army barracks at Fort Moselle.

It was great to sleep in a building on straw mattresses, and we even had electric lights. We cleaned equipment and got replacements, this time from the Air Force, and they were a sorry lot. They hardly knew how to load an M-1 rifle.

We worked hard every day to get all of our gear in shape, but in the afternoon and evening, we could go into Metz proper to wander about, go to bars, or even a movie theater with films in French.

I was thrilled to see the cathedral of Metz, which is very large and very Gothic. We were told it was completed in 1244. What a beautiful piece of architecture it was. There was a Mass for GIs, but I did not get to attend, as I was assigned to a detail that unloaded all the ammo from trucks and hauled it into underground French bunkers for storage and safety. Boy, was it heavy. I thought I must have had a hernia from straining so, carrying those cases of lead shells.

Our mail caught up to us, and I was tickled to receive a box of homemade cookies from my brother John's wife, Lois. She made wonderful cookies, and they were still soft, as she put some apple slices in the box to add moisture.

Although I shared a lot with my squad mates, I saved part of the box, and late at night, I lay in my upper bunk and enjoyed the rest of the cookies. I was warm and dry and resting on a burlap-covered straw mattress. I could even take my boots off. We were out of range of any artillery, and I was in heaven.

Fort Driant, the last fort in Metz still held by the Germans, finally surrendered on December 17, 1944, and now we thought we had it made.

I went across the wooden bridges to get to the downtown section. It was quite a sight to see the big stone arch bridges, each a block apart throughout Metz, that had been blown up by the Germans. The bridges had sunk into the river and looked like so many pancakes. Our Engineers had constructed temporary wooden-truss bridges across at several points, and only foot traffic was allowed.

I ventured into a French movie and had difficulty keeping up with the dialogue, as the French talked so fast. I don't even remember what the movie was about.

After the movie, I went to a nearby pub and sat at a table with four young French teenagers. They were impressed that an American soldier sat with them and that I could speak their language.

They all wanted to see the .45 caliber pistol I was wearing, so I took it out and passed it around the table. I also bought the wine, so I was a small hero. As I got up to go I said, in my best John Wayne manner, *"Je retournner à la guerre,"* I return to the war. They all wished me *"bonne chance,"* (good luck).

As I walked back to the barracks, looking forward to my straw bed, as it began to rain, I noticed feverish activity. I asked someone, "What is going on?"

"Courtney," my sergeant shouted as he saw me, "Where have you been? Get your gear, were moving out!"

Shocked, I ran inside to pack my stuff, and then others told me the Germans had broken through up north and we were heading up there to stop them. Christmas will have to wait.

It took half of the night to get all of the cases of ammo and supplies out of the underground bunkers, where we had so recently carried them. We all loaded on trucks and formed a column and then just sat there in the cold rain. Typical Army, hurry up and wait.

I asked if we could wait inside the barracks, out of the rain. "No!" was the answer. "We are ready to move." In the early dawn of rain and fog, we could make out a jeep with an officer standing on the hood. He would shout to a truckload of men and then would move to the next truck. Finally, he came to our truck.

"The Germans have mounted a big offensive! They have broken

through our lines and overrun a whole division! They are heading for the sea to split the British and American forces. Some Germans are wearing American uniforms and speak English. Because of the bad weather, we have no air support. We are going north until we run into Germans although we don't know where they are! Be Alert!" He then moved on to the next truck.

Cold, wet, and sleepy as we were, we were all shocked to hear this turn of events. We thought we were winning this war. What had happened? Finally the column moved out into the icy wind.

Charlie Campbell was the driver of our truck. He had filled a water can up with wine and was drinking it all night in the rain. As we went over some icy mountains in Belgium he lost control of the truck and was yelling, "Whoopee!" We were pulling a 57 mm antitank, gun and as he swung the wheel, the gun would jackknife and spin the truck sideways. We thought we were going over the side of the mountain and Robbie Robinson, our corporal, kept yelling, "Charlie, cut it out!"

Amazingly, we did not crash and Sgt. Bernie McKittrick got his hands on the wheel. He took over the driver's seat and Charlie fell asleep beside him.

As we entered Belgium, we stopped at a crossroads for a relief break. There was a pub nearby, and our platoon all rushed in. The bartender was so glad to see Americans that he drew beers for everyone. It was one of the finest tasting beers I have ever had. I don't know if it was so much stronger than the weak French beer or just the atmosphere of the moment, but it was great.

During the day, we stopped in Arlon to gas the trucks, and a Belgian woman brought us a pot of hot coffee. The people were all out to cheer us on. They did not want the Germans to come back again.

We entered Luxembourg and got into a pine forest near to where our intelligence told us the enemy might be. We dug in for the night and were very alert on guard. About midnight, Charlie Campbell woke up from his drunk and yelled out, "Robbie!" When Robbie, who was on guard answered, "Here Charlie," Charlie fired his .45 pistol at him. He kept firing until his clip was empty then someone got his gun away from him.

Fortunately, no one was hit, but the next morning, they came and took Charlie to the rear. We never heard from him again. Our platoon sergeant, when he heard the details, said we should have shot him.

We attacked the next day around Bettborn and linked up with our old buddies the 4th Armored Division, along with the 35th and 80th infantry divisions. It was really winter for sure, and we were cold. We fired on some tanks near Dellen but only scared them off, while Vic Martin's gun stopped one tank for good.

Near Merscheid, we came over a snowy hill and took up a gun position to the right of a stone farmhouse. Sgt. Doug Beck put his squad and AT gun across the road and to the left of the barn. A Sherman tank came up from our rear and stopped on the road between the house and barn. Then a truck mounted with quad .50 caliber machine guns pulled up a few yards to the right of our gun.

I remember a rifleman in his foxhole near us saying, "We're getting too much big stuff in here. Always in the past that is when we get it."

He barely finished saying this when, BAM! CARUMPH! the shells started to smash into us. A group of Tiger tanks were coming down the hill from Eschdorf and had discovered our position.

Robbie was kneeling on the frozen ground to sight and fire our 57 mm and I was to his right. I would slam a shell into the breech and yell, "Up! Robbie," which meant the breech block is up - and the gun ready to fire.

In order to see our targets, to yell back the range to us, Sergeant McKittrick, our squad leader, had gone into the shed room on the right side of the farmhouse, and he stood almost level with our gun barrel. When we fired our first round, the muzzle blast knocked him backward and off his feet.

He came running outside and took a new position behind a tree to our right. There was a lot of noise and confusion and then screaming. Beck's gun took a direct hit and was out of action with dead and wounded all around. VanNorman and Beck loaded the wounded on their truck and headed back over the hill to our rear.

The Sherman tank was firing at the Germans as I went into the house with Johnnie Humphries, a medic. He seemed to be exhausted.

I sat on a couch against the wall next to the road with Johnnie, and he was telling me that his nerves were frazzled from patching up guys.

Just then we heard a yell, "Medic! Medic!" from outside.

Johnnie said, "Well here we go again," and he got up and headed out through the kitchen to go outside. After a moment, I thought to myself, I might as well go too.

Just as I got to the kitchen, WHAMMO! A shell crashed through the wall and destroyed the living room we had just left. Another shell hit the Sherman tank and we could hear screams.

The guys climbed up on the tank and found one man inside who was alive. They pulled him out and his one leg was dangling and the foot and ankle were spinning around, held on by a piece of flesh. He was placed on the floor of the kitchen, and the medic cut off the dangling foot with a bayonet.

The injured soldier was awake but in shock. He looked up at me and asked if I would go out to the tank and get his musette bag, which was tied to the outside of the turret.

I said, "Man you don't know what you are asking."

He said, "Please, Mac, it's important to me."

So I went outside the farmhouse and the tank was on fire. The cases of bullets stored on the back of the tank were shooting all over the place. Other GIs who were huddled behind the stone wall of the house said, "Courtney, don't go out there to the tank."

I had promised, so I went, climbed up on the side of the tank, pulled out my trench knife, and cut the musette bag loose. Just after I jumped to the ground and ran back to the house, the whole tank exploded in a ball of fire.

When I gave the bag to the wounded GI, I said to him, "I hope what you want in this bag is really important, as I almost got it out there." He said, "Yeah, it was. I had my last pair of dry socks in there." Poor guy.

It was here that we were firing at the oncoming armor, when I yelled to Bailey and McGregor, "More ammo! Hurry!" They were trying to break open the wooden ammo boxes with bayonets because the metal clasps were frozen shut with ice. Each time they got a box open they would scream, "No ammo!"

What had happened was that when we were in Saar-Union, France, we found a warehouse full of cognac. We thought we would stock up for the winter, so we took the 57 mm shells out of the cardboard casings and inserted bottles of cognac, which just fit. We put the cases into the boxes and loaded the cognac shells at the bottom of the load of shells on the truck. The 57 mm shells we hid under the hay in a French barn.

As it happened, there in Luxembourg, we had cases of cognac but no ammo. All of the other GIs had gone over the snowy hill behind us. We thought we should leave the gun and run back as well. McGregor came up with an idea to run the winch line around the big tree and pull the gun around the tree and drop it off a five foot wall. It sure did bounce but the gun came free. We hooked the gun to the truck, and Ronnie took off to the rear. We decided to go on foot instead of in the truck. All the way back running in the snow, I thought I could feel holes in my back as the Germans sprayed the area around us with machine gun fire.

None of our squad got hit, and we gathered together in a house on the other side of the hill. We figured the German tankers would be along any minute, and we had very little to shoot with. Then we remembered, it was Christmas Eve! McKittrick had grabbed two bottles of cognac, so we passed these around and wished each other Merry Christmas. To our surprise and relief, the Germans did not come. They stayed in Eschdorf for the night. Maybe they had a Christmas celebration too.

It did not occur to me until years later that running out of ammunition and finding only bottles of cognac in the shell cases may have saved our lives.

Since the German tanks had knocked out our other 57 mm antitank gun, the quad .50 caliber machine gun truck, and the Sherman tank, our gun was the only one left. If we had been able to keep firing, the Germans would have kept coming until they knocked us out too.

Once we stopped firing, they probably assumed they had eliminated all the enemy on the flank and retired back into Eschdorf for the night. It was one of those quirks of warfare that are not planned but just happen. In this case, I am glad that we camouflaged the cognac and took it along, even though we ended up leaving most of the full bottles back in the snow.

Christmas Day we had a real fight in Eschdorf, complete with aerial dogfights overhead. I set up our .50 caliber machine gun on a tripod in the barnyard to shoot at the Me-109s that were strafing us. Pinky Piquette, our platoon sergeant, told me that I would only last about two minutes on that gun. On the next strafing run, the Me-109 was attacked by a P-47, and after a brief dogfight, the German shot down the P-47 and it crashed about one mile from us.

We got into a house on the main street of Eschdorf with a mother and three little children. I could speak French with her and wished her and the children a Joyeux Noël. Wyndham "Bill" Owen played with the kids and said they reminded him of his own kids back home in Scranton, Pennsylvania.

After dark, a GI came down the street and said there would be a Catholic Mass in the church at 8:00 P.M. One from each squad could go. Sgt. Vic Martin and I plus Joe Lieb, the jeep driver of our platoon, went up the hill to the church.

Inside it was all dark, except for the stars overhead, as the roof had been blown off by our artillery. The chaplain had two candles lit on the altar, and a tanker played the organ. We all sang those Christmas hymns, "Adeste Fideles," "Silent Night," and "O Little Town of Bethlehem." I must have been dreaming of home as I fell asleep sitting up. Vic Martin had to jab me awake when it was time to receive Holy Communion.

I never knew the priest's name but he said, "You men will remember this Christmas Mass for the rest of your lives." He was right. I have never forgotten and relive it every Christmas. For many men they did not have long to remember, as many died in the next few weeks in the Ardennes forests.

My mother used to write poems, so a few days later, when I got a chance to send a letter home, I wrote her the following poem:

Christmas Night
I Can't Tell Where

All was quiet on the battle front, the sentries were on guard,
The distant guns like thunder, filled the air;
The Moon was shining brightly on the snow covered ground
It was Christmas night—I can't tell where.
It was Christmas—we were dreaming of so many other years,
And of comrades we had loved that were no more;
When a G.I. passing by spoke that all around could hear:—
Mass at 8:15 in Church, that touched the core.
It echoed like the bugler's call and was answered just the same
Boys came from fox holes, houses and from tanks;
As the villagers looked out upon the snow clad, moonlit street,
They could see that small procession of us Yanks.
The Church, we found was blacked out but the altar
blazed with candles,
A tanker played the hymns we knew so well;
There was no choir leader, yet we sang with an accord
Our eyes were wet with tears I have to tell.
The Mass, of course, was beautiful, the sermon too, was grand
Nearly everyone of us received Communion;
In growing up, I'm sure we never fully realized
The beauty of the Catholic Church's Union.
The Mass, too soon, was finished, the last prayers had been said
We wiped our eyes and started for the door
Our spirits had been lifted, but as we left the Church
We heaved a sigh and went back to the war.

When we got back to our platoon area, we were told to leave our gun in place, that we were going to fight as line soldiers. We formed a single file and headed off down into a deep valley on the north side of Eschdorf. It was cold and crystal clear in the moonlight, as we walked and slid on the ice down into this deep ravine.

Many men slipped and fell on the patches of ice, but no one cried out as we quietly descended into the gorge.

At the bottom, there was a very small village of a dozen or so houses surrounded on three sides by steep banks covered with trees. The Germans must have climbed up the steep banks to escape, as we only found one dead paratrooper on the road into the village. He was used that night as a reference point when passing out directions, "Turn left at the dead paratrooper."

It got so bitter cold as we got into the houses that we decided to light a fire in a pot-bellied stove. The wood box was empty, so I went out back, found some small logs and a bowsaw, and started to saw up some firewood.

It was so quiet that the saw made an awful racket in the cold night air and seemed to echo in the little valley. I thought to myself that if the Krauts were still up there on the steep hillside, all they would have to do was drop grenades and they would fall on us. None did, but the very thought made me saw faster.

We barely got the fire lit, when we got orders to move out. Back up the long icy path to Eschdorf again. Each man was quietly thinking to himself, "I wonder what they are doing at home this Christmas night. Bet everyone is stuffed with turkey dinner and is gathered around a warm fireplace."

Joe Lieb told me later that when he drove his jeep down the steep trail, he slid on the ice, so when he drove back up the hill, he made sure to gun the engine and go high up on the ice bank to allow for the slide. He told "Shorty" Mrowinsky to do the same, but Shorty forgot and he slid and the jeep overturned into a ravine. Shorty jumped free and walked up the trail. The next day, he went down again and was able to right the jeep and drive it back.

When we got back to Eschdorf the next morning, there had been an artillery barrage and the house we had been in with the woman and her three little children was a mass of stones and rubble. I never did know if they got out or were buried under that rubble.

There was a wooden shed at the end of the street still standing and, being curious, I opened up the door to find dozens of frozen GIs stacked up like cordwood. I quietly closed the shed door.

Private Courtney with his father, Frank, at Altoona, Pennsylvania, on last furlough before shipping out, May 1944.

Captured photograph of German attack dogs similar to Smokey, the dog Duquette acquired.

Captured photograph of German antitank gun showing how easily the crew can maneuver it since it is so well balanced.

YD riflemen in Belgium counterattacking during the Battle of the Bulge, here helping repel German thrusts at Bastogne. From *The History of the 26th Yankee Division, 1917–1919, 1941–1945*, copyright 1955 by Yankee Division Veterans Association, reproduced by permission of the Association.

Column of 104th Regiment infantrymen in winter in Luxembourg, where the Germans mounted some of the most vicious attacks of the war. From *The History of the 26th Yankee Division*, reproduced by permission.

Exhausted in the fighting near Wiltz, Luxembourg, two GIs rest for a moment on a snow-encrusted ammunition box in the woods in the combat area. From *The History of the 26th Yankee Division*, reproduced by permission.

Plaque outside church at Eschdorf, Luxembourg, honoring men of the 26th Infantry Division who fought in this sector during the Battle of the Ardennes, 1944–45. Photograph by Capt. Christopher Courtney.

Bridge at Saarlautern, Germany. From the *YD Grapevine*, October 21, 1945.

Street-to-street, house-to-house fighting in Saarlautern, one of the most stubbornly defended cities the YD encountered. From *The History of the 26th Yankee Division*, reproduced by permission.

Larry Choiniere (in fore-
ground) dancing to the tune of
a "liberated" guitar played by
Sam Harper as Edward
"Robbie" Robinson looks on,
Germany, Spring 1945.

Left to right: Lt. John Deviese
and Lt. Ernest Tripp, Germany,
Spring 1945.

Postcard showing headquarters of the 3rd Battalion in Potsmühle, Czechoslovakia. The dance hall is to the left.

Private Courtney on guard duty in Potsmühle, July 1945, with two little friends.

Art Schwartz (with sidearm) and Private Courtney.
Wettern, Czechoslovakia, July 1945.

Private Courtney outside schoolhouse, Wettern, July 1945.

Sketch of Private Courtney, done by Wilhem Zawischa at Bad Schallerbach, Austria, September 20, 1945.

Postcard depicting entrance to Scharding, Austria, 1945.

Recent (1995) photograph of Český Krumlov, Czech Republic, showing Castle (tower and series of long buildings to the right) from the northeast. During the war, this town was known as Krummau. Photograph courtesy of the Executive Director of the Town Hall, Český Krumlov.

Edward "Robbie" Robinson beside statue of Joan of Arc, Reims, France, November 1945.

Unidentified Parisienne
photographed on the Champs-
Elysées by Private Courtney,
November 13, 1945.

Left ot right: JoePuchalski, Ron McGregor, and Robert "Tex" VanNorman
at Fort Dix, New Jersey, separation center, January 1, 1946.

The GIs assigned to pick up the dead bodies were called GROs, Graves Registration Orderlies. They would show up following any heavy action to remove all dead bodies, both American and German.

The GRO men became so used to dead bodies that they no longer thought of them as GIs. They would work in pairs to pick up corpses, one man at the head and one man at the feet. They would pick up the body and swing it up in the air to land on the truck or back of a jeep.

Sometimes they would sing as they worked, gruesome as it sounds. If they happened to be retrieving bodies when their GI comrades were still in the area, they would get screamed at with threats by the GIs to "stop that singing and lift those men up with respect!"

No one could stand by and see his buddy, who had been alive a short time ago, thrown up on a truck as so much cordwood. The GROs had to get hardened to their work.

One of the duties of the GRO was to remove the "dog tags" from around the neck of the dead soldier. One dog tag was placed in the body's mouth to stay with the body for identification. The other dog tag was used to compile lists of the dead.

Each soldier was issued a pair of identification tags named "dog tags" by GI humor. Stamped into the metal was the soldier's first name, middle initial and last name, followed by his Army serial number of eight digits, then the dates of his last tetanus shots (mine showed T 43 & 44) and last item to the right, his blood type (mine was "O").

Below this it had the name and home address of the next of kin, and the last item appeared in the lower right corner. A "C" for Catholic or a "P" for Protestant. I never saw any, but I imagine they had a "J" for Jewish or "H" for Hebrew and "M" for Muslim and maybe others.

We secured our gun to the truck and moved through curving hills to drop down to a winding river valley. The Sûre River cut a deep gorge in a series of twisting curves until we came to the old medieval village of Esch-sur-Sûre. The Germans had blown the center out of the stone arch structure of the only bridge over the Sûre. Our Engineers soon placed a Bailey Bridge over the remaining piers, and we occupied the town.

It was bitter cold and the Sûre River had chunks of ice floating in it. The steep banks were icy and frozen with snow. We were glad we did not have to ford that river and were grateful to the Engineers who constructed the Bailey Bridge which was a steel structure that reminded us of an Erector Set. Each section of steel truss was complete and had to be swung across a span with a crane and bolted together. Often this was done under fire and took a lot of courage to do.

A month or so later, we heard there was a story that General Patton came up to the bank of the river at Esch-sur-Sûre and asked for a GI volunteer to swim the river and scout the enemy on the other side. He is reputed to have offered a three-day pass to Paris for anyone who did it. Ha! We all laughed in derision.

First, we did not see Patton at Esch-sur-Sûre, and if he did offer a three day pass as a reward, no one would be foolish enough to try to swim that river. He would freeze to death before reaching the other bank, much less, scout the enemy and then swim back.

Such stories were often fabricated by war correspondents to flatter the generals and to affect the morale on the home front. To the GI "Willie and Joes," they were good for a laugh.

That night we were so hungry for something other than our cold K-rations of cheese and rye-krisp crackers that I went out after dark and sneaked into a hen house and came back with four chickens. I learned how to grab a chicken by the neck so fast that it would not give out a squeak. Then I would twist off its head and put the chicken body in a cloth bag I found.

Our squad ate well that night, which we said was our belated Christmas dinner. Phil Fox said he would call me "Dick the chicken killer." As I said, I had become our squad scrounger.

During most of the war, our platoon was always forward and never near our kitchen. We often wondered if Joe Sorrentino, our mess sergeant, stayed back in Normandy, as we never saw him until later. Most of the time we ate K- or C-rations and sometimes 10 in 1 rations, which were much better. The 10 in 1 rations even had some caramels or Milky Ways in them.

The 10 in 1 rations were supposedly meals for 10 men in 1 box. Each box was fastened with a half-inch metal band which, could be snapped open with a bayonet or trench knife.

We were glad to get the little packs of toilet paper (tan colored) in the Ks but would rather have had a chocolate bar instead. One of my postwar ambitions was to find that committee of nutrition specialists that chose the dry, hard crackers for K-rations and force them to eat that stuff for a week.

Our 3rd Battalion command post was set up in the little hillside town of Kaundorf, while our platoon moved on to Buderscheid, a small crossroads village. Here I captured a very cold German and liberated his wristwatch. He was too cold to fight and just wanted to get out of that field of snow. At last our squad had a watch so that we could time our guard watch at night. Before this, we had to guess when each man's two hours were up, which caused a lot of dissension as nobody believed it was time yet to wake up.

We got into a house right near the crossroad and Sgt. Vic Martin housed his squad across the road in a corner *Gasthaus*. We received a lot of mortar fire, and after one barrage, we heard a scream from Vic Martin's house.

I yelled "That's Vic!" and Sgt. Bernie McKittrick and I started to run across a snowy field toward the road next to Vic's location. I was a few paces ahead of Bernie and ran smack into a rusty barbed wire fence which snapped in two. In my excitement I did not know that the fence had ripped open my chest.

When we arrived at the door to the *Gasthaus,* we found a GI with his legs shattered. He was just coming out of the door when the shell hit right through the door.

Vic Martin was frying up some eggs on a kitchen stove a few feet away but was not hit. Four of us picked up the wounded man, from K Company I think, and carried him about two hundred yards to a forward aid station.

He kept screaming, "Oh God! I'm going! I know I'm going!" We tried to run, but the road was so icy we almost dropped him, and we even got tangled up in some wire on the road.

Shortly after we got him to the medic, he died from loss of blood. When the medic saw the blood on my chest he asked where I was hit, I said I wasn't. Then I looked down and for the first time realizing that I had tangled with the barbed wire fence. "I'm O.K., just scratched."

One of the medics wanted to list me to get a Purple Heart but I said no. When I saw the man lying there on the floor with his legs blown off, dead, I thought it would be unfair for me to get a Purple Heart for a scratch.

When I got back to my squad, we were told to move up the road towards Wiltz. We had two replacements in our squad who had just arrived two days before and who knew nothing about a 57 mm anti-tank gun or bazooka. They were griping about everything since they arrived, and we never even got their names.

As we moved up the valley road under fire, we crouched behind a curve in the road for cover behind some big rocks. Machine gun fire raked the snow in the road. We got the word, "Let's go!" and prepared to move out around the big rocks.

The two replacements started yelling for Sergeant Piquette, our platoon sergeant. Pinky appeared all red-faced from running and one of these men said, "Sergeant, we are not going up that road!"

"What do you mean you aren't?" shouted Pinky Piquette.

"All I know is that we are not going up that road!"

We were shocked to hear this and then Pinky said "O.K., then come with me," and he led them to the rear. We never saw or heard about them ever again.

At first we were sort of mad. "What about us? We aren't thrilled to go up that road," we all mumbled to each other. Finally, we all went up the road thinking we are glad those two are gone. Sure wouldn't want to have to depend on those guys in a tight spot.

It got colder and colder as we mixed in with I Company on the road. At a three-way crossroads we got held up and dug in foxholes just to keep warm, or so we thought. One of the guys from I Company grabbed my shovel and said, "Let me dig awhile so I can get warm."

It was here I dug one of the worst holes I dug in the whole war and at the worst spot—a crossroads. We were always trained to avoid crossroads because the Krauts had them zeroed in and could drop mortar rounds or 88 mm shells right on the spot.

Little did I know that we would be pinned down there for the next sixteen days under constant shelling. I dug into the hillside of a ditch and built a roof of poles and branches of pine to keep out the snow, but the front of the hole facing the enemy was open to the cold, and I really had very little protection. I should have dug deeper into the side of the hill, but the ground was frozen so hard and the weather so cold. I just did not feel like digging.

We were pinned there so long that we thought the war had passed and forgotten us. If a jeep came up from Buderscheid, it was a quick stop to drop off a case of K-rations and some ammo and then beat a hasty path to the rear. We began to feel abandoned.

McKittrick and Ronnie McGregor made a hole in the ditch and placed logs over it. One dark night a tank came up the road, and when the shells started to land it backed up over their hole. They were inside screaming as the logs cracked, but somehow they held. We all pulled the logs off and got them out after the tank went to the rear.

We fought the weather as much as the Germans. We could not have any fires even in daylight as the atmosphere was so dark and foggy it would give away our position if the Krauts saw the light of a fire. So we ate cold K-rations, cheese and crackers, pork and egg yolk. We usually took care of any bowel needs at night and in a hurry. We didn't seem to need to go very often because of the cold, little food, and tension.

One day the jeep dropped off something new called heat tablets. Little gray blocks that when lit gave off heat but no light. I melted snow in my canteen cup and made coffee. It was wonderful! Later I burned a hole right through my boot as I did not realize the heat tablet was still burning. What a time for a hotfoot.

After so long under fire, you begin to ignore the danger or else become so used to it that you become careless. I remember running out from my hole to pick up some metal can lids to line the roof of my foxhole. Ron McGregor was in his hole watching me. He said, "Old Courtney doesn't care if he gets hit or not."

I said, "Don't worry. I count the seconds." We could hear this one artillery piece as it fired and counted the seconds until the shell landed near us. I knew how many seconds I had before I had to dive back into my hole.

Sgt. Vic Martin's squad was dug in along the road about 75 yards to our rear. Some mornings I would run or crawl down the ditch to visit Vic and "Ciangi" and Leroy Unverferth. It was good to talk and check on who all was still alive.

One morning, I awoke so stiff and cold that I did not go down to visit Vic's hole. That afternoon, Sergeant Piquette arrived in a jeep with Joe Lieb and dove in my hole as an artillery barrage hit us. We both had our faces pushed into the ground as the shells karoompfed all around us. When the shelling slowed up a little, Pinky told me that Vic's hole had taken a direct hit from a mortar. Vic and Roy were both badly wounded but alive. Ciancaglini, my buddy, was dead.

Later that day, I took a chance and ran back to their hole, which had the top logs blown off and the shelter half hanging loose over the hole. I pulled up the shelter half, and there was Ciangi in the same corner of the hole where he always sat. His glasses were smashed, and a trickle of blood ran out of his mouth and froze. I made the sign of the cross and said a prayer for my buddy and ran back up the road to my hole.

After I got safely back in my hole, I sat there quietly thinking about my friends. Wonder how bad Vic and Leroy were hurt? Pinky had said only that they were hit and evacuated to Buderscheid.

I remember how, on the ship coming over, Ciangi had asked, "How many of us will come back?"

Well, Ciangi won't be back home again. What will his family do when they learn of his death? I wish I could tell them that he was always faithful to his Catholic faith. Then I realized that I did not even know his home address.

Then I started to worry about how the GRO men could find his body. The foxhole was sunk in a roadside ditch and now all covered with snow. If there is time, you should fix a dead man's bayonet on the muzzle of his M-1 rifle then jam the bayonet into the ground and place his helmet on top of the rifle butt to signify the location of a dead body.

But Ciangi did not have an M-1 rifle. He was armed with a carbine, which is shorter and cannot have a bayonet attached. What if no one finds him? What can I do?

Finally, I had to shake myself loose from those thoughts. If you dwell on them too long, you can go nuts. I consoled myself by praying for the repose of his soul. He was such a good man. My buddy was gone.

We had been told that the Germans had some troops wearing American uniforms and speaking English. We did not trust anyone we did not know and asked many questions of strangers like who married Betty Grable? What team did Lou Gehrig play for? It was a time of great uncertainty.

That night it snowed heavily with big silent flakes. We were right on the edge of a dense forest, and the road ran right into it. I was on guard duty for our squad about 1:00 A.M. and as I sat there with my carbine in my lap, I got sleepy and dozed off. I awoke with a start to sense, more than see, several men on the road a few yards away from my hole.

I shouted "Halt!" They stopped. One of them in a deep voice yelled to me, "Stay awake, Mac! Stay awake!" and they went off down the road. I often wonder still if that guy was German or American. I'll never know.

On the day that we first came to this crossroads, we looked at a gun position across the field to our left along the edge of the woods. It was sort of dug-in, almost made to order, as if it had been used before.

Pinky and McKittrick decided that our field of fire would not be able to cover down the road and also that our escape route would be cut off if we had to abandon the position in a hurry. That is how we ended up right on the crossroads, which we all thought would only be temporary.

The Germans had mapped this area very well, and I feel certain that they thought an American antitank crew would choose that same spot in the field as a gun position. My idea was confirmed one afternoon, when under a heavy barrage, I peeked out of my hole to see a concentration of shells landing right smack on the spot we would have been dug in if we had chosen the field position.

I also think that the Germans knew that we were not green troops and that we had learned from bitter experience not to dig in or even tarry long on any crossroads. Therefore, I think that may be the reason that they did not concentrate artillery or mortar fire on the crossroads itself. I guess this is one time that disobeying the rules of warfare saved our lives. Or else it was just dumb luck.

To our surprise, one afternoon a jeep drove leisurely up from the rear, instead of the hurried approach usually used by our supply jeeps whose drivers were aware of the regular artillery and mortar fire. At the crossroads two officers got out, immaculately dressed with shiny boots and creases in their uniforms.

They started to walk up the hill on the right fork, and one GI yelled from his foxhole, "Sir, you better take cover. We are about due for another barrage."

"Don't worry soldier. We just want to look around up here." They kept going up the road.

As the GI predicted, the shelling began. A few minutes later a helmet rolled down the road with the officer's head in it. No one knew what happened to the other officer or even who they were. Meanwhile, when the shells started to land, the jeep and driver raced back to the rear at more than a leisurely pace.

"Pee Wee" Moore, who was a brand new replacement from the States, when he heard some machine gun fire, yelled, "Maybe we should go and help those guys out?" He was new and wanted to shoot someone.

We yelled, "No! Stay put in your hole but keep your eyes open!"

The Germans switched to phosphorous shells, which left a haze of smoke and this awful pungent odor that hung in the forest for days. The smell was awful and the fumes burned your nose, eyes, and throat. We could imagine how it would burn our skin if it had hit us.

Sometimes we would crawl out of our own foxholes and get into the hole of another member of our squad. One day I was lying proneright outside the hole of Bernie McKittrick and Ron McGregor. I said, "Remember the slogan used to be, 'Victory in '43?' Then it became 'Win the war in '44!' Well, now I figure we ought to change it to 'Stay alive in '45!'"

Slowly the days and nights passed. At any moment a mortar round would drop, or an 88 mm shell would arrive, later a full barrage. Then dense smoke and fog would follow along with periods of silence, while big white flakes of snow piled up and then drifted with the wind.

By now, most of our squad had grown beards or stubble whiskers. Everyone looked dirty and ragged. No one had a haircut in a month. I was "the kid" because I did not have much of a beard to shave. My hair had grown down over my ears, though, which helped against the cold. No war correspondent got up this far to take our pictures. We might have scared the home folks if they had.

I never took my boots off, much less my clothes. We wore the same clothes day and night usually for six weeks or more. When I could get a dry pair of socks I would change them. Sometimes whenever I did, the old socks were in tatters and pieces around my ankles.

We were told not to lace our boots too tight as we might get trench foot. Some guys were going to go ahead and lace them tighter so they would get trench foot because the rumor was that they would send you back to the States for treatment.

Our Army was not well equipped for winter combat. We did not have hoods, or heavy scarves or wristwarmer sleeves like they have today. The tankers used to have hoods, but the doughfoot never got any issued to him.

For the winter, I wore a pair of long-john underwear, wool uniform pants and shirt, a wool sweater plus a tie (that General Patton insisted upon), regular weight socks (usually tried to wear two pairs at once), combat boots, a combat jacket, a wool knit skullcap which was too skimpy to cover the ears, a helmet liner, and steel helmet. Worst of all were the gloves. They were unlined, plain, one-ply wool and they were always wet or frozen stiff. We needed heavy canvas gloves that were waterproof and lined for warmth.

Many times I would remember that when I was a senior back at Altoona Catholic High School, the girls in the class would be knitting long woolen scarves to be sent to soldiers through the Red Cross. Maybe they were all sent to troops in the South Pacific as we never saw any, or maybe the GIs in Paris were wearing them.

In a letter from my brother Bill, who was an Infantry captain in the South Pacific, he said, "I have seen pictures of you guys in the snow. I don't know how you can operate in that climate." We didn't know how either, but we did it anyhow.

Bill did not know it, but I wondered how they could operate in the jungle with dense foliage, bugs, disease, and snakes. While we suffered in the cold, I could imagine him in the steamy heat.

I remember that during our basic training, all they talked about were the Japanese. They never told us how to fight Germans. One day, they even taught us a few words of Japanese, but again, no German. So here we are in Europe. *C'est la guerre.*

We used to console ourselves that for the next war we would make our fortune by designing combat uniforms and plenty of extra pairs of socks and lots of gun-patches for cleaning our weapons. There never seemed to be enough of those.

We also had a canvas shelter half and wool blanket plus a wool overcoat. We did not wear our overcoats because they were so bulky and hindered you from rapid movements. The only time I ever put on my overcoat was the night we left Luxembourg by truck and drove all night in bitter wind.

I used to tell myself that I would always remember this particular hole at "88 Junction," as we called our crossroads. Spending so many days there, about sixteen in all, I got to know every branch and twig that I had laced together to support the walls and roof where I could see the metal lids, that looked like garbage can lids, which I had woven among the pine branches to keep out the falling snow. Only the good Lord protected me from falling 88s and mortar shells. One may wonder why I did not dig deeper and put heavy logs and dirt over the hole, but it was just too cold to care. Maybe if I had tried to, I might have been out of the hole dragging a log and been hit by shrapnel. Who knows?

I had plenty of time to think and plenty of time to pray, and I did a lot of both.

None of us knew how many men from our batallion were killed or wounded at the "crossroads," but we knew there were a lot. Some of them we knew from our time together in the States. Maybe we had a beer with them at the PX or in town. Others, we never even learned their names, as they arrived as replacements and were killed soon after.

I felt sorry for the ones who were hurriedly rushed up to the front from Paris where they had been typists or office clerks at the rear echelon headquarters. They came right from a warm bed to a frigid forest where they learned to dig a hole in the ground fast. Some did not learn to dig fast enough.

One man I saw tried to load an M-1 rifle clip of ammo from the bottom of the breech instead of from the top. It was pitiful. Some men froze to death because their bodies were not accustomed to living out in subzero temperatures.

The German thrust through Luxembourg and Belgium nearly succeeded. Our High Command was caught off-guard and desperately had to throw in any man that could be found to stop the German advance. Even wounded men who could hold a weapon were often returned to the front as soon as they were treated.

This was a battle that was not in the textbooks. What stopped the Germans was the individual courage and resourcefulness of each American GI.

Where Germans were so well trained to obey that they would often hold up movement until they got orders, Americans would often size up the situation and act on what their common sense told them to do. Most of the Battle of the Bulge was fought by small groups such as platoons or even squads on their own.

The Germans were better trained and had better equipment, but the Americans had more equipment. We had initiative and good old American ingenuity.

Our army too had some slackers and cowards. Some men shot themselves in the foot to get out of action. For the most part, though, everyone knew what we were fighting for and they knew that everyone at home supported us. We just wanted to win the war and then go home.

Praise the Lord! One day our platoon sergeant, Pinky, drove up in a jeep and calmly told us we could move out. The Krauts had been pinched off across our front which relieved the pressure on us. Wow! We had survived. We jumped on the truck and did not even look back as we pulled away. There were a lot fewer of us now than when we first got here.

We went into the town of Arsdorf and lived in houses while we got reequipped with weapons, ammo, and replacements for our losses. I was transferred to Vic Martin's former first squad, and Paul "Jake" Lipps from Bradford, Pennsylvania, was the squad sergeant. Jake was the CQ (Charge of Quarters) in the orderly room at Camp Campbell, Kentucky, when I first transferred to the 26th Division on New Year's Eve 1943. He said he would try to get me into the antitank platoon, which he did.

We got to see a movie here and were each issued five American candy bars. We thought the war must be over.

Beck's 3rd squad had lost its 57 mm gun to a direct hit, and until it could be replaced, we had picked up a captured 88 mm gun which Sgt. Beck planned to use. We tried it out in a field, and the roar of the gun shook us up. We all agreed it was a good weapon. It had sure thrown enough stuff at us.

By comparison to the German 88 mm our 57 mm gun was a suicide weapon. It did not have the power to penetrate the armor on a German tank. We had to hit them on the sides or on the rear, maybe a lucky shot to the underside if a tank was coming up over a rise. The muzzle blast of the 57 mm was just like a red line showing where we were in position. The 88 mm had a muzzle brake on the front of the barrel.

The 88 mm could also be raised to a higher trajectory and used as artillery or all the way up to be an antiaircraft weapon. It was very versatile.

We discussed, while getting acquainted with the 88 mm, that it had wonderful balance. One man could pick up the end of the trails and, on level ground, move the gun around. Our 57 mm was not well balanced and required two men to lift the heavy trails and at least one man to lie down on the barrel to offset some of the weight.

The 57 mm was unwieldy and the 88 mm was easier to move around. Thus, the Germans could fire a round and quickly move to a new position. We took more effort, and at least one man was more exposed to fire as he went forward to lie down on the barrel.

We next took Baulaide and Fleboun where our artillery TOT (time on target) barrage had turned a forest into what looked like a toothpick factory. Then we took Bavigne, just another town in the snow and cold. When would we run out of towns in the snow to be taken?

At Mon-Schurmann we had a lot of casualties due to Teller mines. These were round metal explosive devices that looked like pie plates. They are buried in the road and covered with dirt to conceal them. When enough weight is placed on the mine, such as a jeep or tank, it depresses the detonator that explodes the mine.

The only defense is to crawl along the road and try to locate the mines and remove them. This is easier said than done, particularly if you are exposed to enemy fire while you are doing it.

As we next passed through Winseler, to our surprise, we came upon a civilian funeral procession. There was a fancy carved funeral carriage, drawn by two black horses, with a coffin aboard but no flowers. It seemed so out of place. With so many dead soldiers, both German and American out in the snow, here was a small village going about the business of honoring one of its own. As we passed by, we felt like interlopers and those in the procession looked at us as if to say, "Move on," which is what we did.

As we moved through another outfit in Neider-Wiltz, we saw a group of reinforcements fresh from the States. You could always spot them by the new helmets and uniforms. When we started to move forward to follow our artillery fire, one of the new guys yelled in a loud voice, "Don't worry boys, I'll soon be up there." Poor guy, I thought. He doesn't know what he is in for. By now I felt like an old-timer. I had reason to.

We finally entered Wiltz, our objective, after fighting so long. In a way we were kind of disappointed. After all, it was just another town. Weren't they all "just another town?"

The generals and staff officers must know the strategic importance of certain road junctions like Wiltz and Bastogne, but to the ordinary infantryman it is just another town.

An old woman called me into her cellar and gave me a drink of schnapps. She told me how long she had waited for us to return. She showed me a picture of an American soldier that she had hidden from the Heinies when they had retaken Wiltz during the Battle of the Bulge. She said the Germans had treated the civilians so badly that they lived in terror and were afraid to go outside.

Later that day, we moved into a house where we were met by a feisty little old man who could speak good English. "You tell your Captain that I want no looting here! Do you understand? No looting!"

We all admired his guts and we did not touch anything in his home. We also wondered if he talked that way to the Germans? Ha!

When we checked the second floor we were surprised to see that there was indoor plumbing! Most of the houses in France did not have it. However, when we looked in the bathroom, the bathtub and the pedestal sink were mounded full of human excretions which had frozen to a bluish gray. It was quite a sight to behold.

We guessed that the civilians or German soldiers had not dared go outside either due to cold or our artillery fire, or both. We decided to pick another house for our squad that night.

In a few days, we were told to be ready to move out, back to the south where we came from. But there was a new twist. Men came around with cans of OD paint and painted over the "26DIV" on all the jeeps, trucks, tanks, etc. We were told to remove all of our blue YD patches we wore on our left shoulder sleeves. Also, we had to go through any letters we had received and tear off the address to "APO 26." Anything that mentioned the 26th Division had to go. Why? We were going to disappear. The 26th Division would fall off the map in the eyes of the Germans.

We turned in all of our YD patches and had to show our mail for inspection that no 26 was in view. Then we were issued 95th Division patches to sew on our sleeves (as if we all carried needle and thread).

Our vehicles showed 95 where the 26 had been painted over. Also the 104th Regiment numbers were painted out. If captured, we were to be the men of the 95th.

While this may have been a good ruse to confuse the Germans, it sure made us mad. We were very proud of the 26th YD, and we did not want to wear another outfit's designation. I often wondered if it did fool any Germans.

On a bitter cold night, we loaded the trucks and the whole division headed south. We backtracked over much of the territory we fought for, and this time we drove right through the heart of Luxembourg City, the capital. We saw the government headquarters buildings and the city and then moved on out of Luxembourg.

Our job here was finished and another chapter had been written in the history of the old YD, a chapter written in blood on the white snows of one of the smallest countries in Europe.

What was the next mission? Had we earned a rest or did the High Command have another job waiting for us? We would soon know. We hunkered down in the back of the truck to try to escape the cold wind as the caravan crunched its way southward.

5

Cellars of Saarlautern

AT 1750 HOURS ON THE 27TH OF JANUARY 1945, we crossed the border and entered the "holy soil" of Germany. How long we had aimed for this!

We entered what was left of the sizable city of Saarlautern (now known as Saarlouis). We crunched through the streets of rubble and found a row of buildings where we could shelter for the night. It was cold with a raw dampness in the air.

Our squad had liberated a small barrel stove that we brought with us on the truck. We carried it in, unhooked the big stove in the room, and hooked up our small one to the pipes because it heated up much faster. We learned to carry this stove along to use it whenever we could.

One hardly got used to the darkness every night. We would have to pick our way over rubble of bricks, mortar, and household items all strewn about. Doing so at night seemed to make a lot more noise, and we feared that we would give away our position. It was always a problem.

Still wearing our 95th Division shoulder patch insignias, we were here to replace the 95th, which had secured a bridgehead across the Saar River. The Germans had ordered all the civilians to evacuate the city and it was a ghost town except for the German troops set in their pillboxes on the eastern section of the city across the river.

The 3rd Battalion was to cross over the only American-held bridge and replace the 379th Infantry Regiment on the salient near the railroad station. We were warned to go fast when we crossed the bridge as it was under good observation and heavy fire by the Krauts. The long approach run to the bridge gave the German gunners ample notice of our rush to cross. The hair stood up on the back of our necks as we took our turns to get across the bridge.

Our 3rd Battalion CP moved in to a German pillbox, and the anti-tank platoon set up our guns to the right next to what was left of several houses. We did not have to dig in as we lived in the cellars under the smashed houses.

While 104th Regiment headquarters lived pretty good back across the river in old army barracks and apartments, we were up on the bridge-head where the Germans were just across the narrow cobblestone street from us in their cellars.

It was a miserable time of wet, sloppy weather and the dreary, dank smell of the cellars. We kept pretty quiet during the day, but patrols probed back and forth across the streets every night.

Some of our platoon, since there was virtually no armored activity, were moved up to augment the line companies as riflemen. We took turns standing guard in the front rooms of the destroyed houses facing the Germans. We could see German patrols come along, look into the house, and move on. I always expected that some night they might throw a "potato masher," what we called a German hand grenade, through the open window frame of the room where I was. So one day two of us found a piece of chicken coop wire and tacked it across the window frame.

Only two nights later, I was there on guard when a German threw a grenade that hit the wire barrier and bounced back into the street and exploded right next to him. The next morning his body was still lying there in the broken bricks.

I used to hate it when we had to leave the comparative safety of the cellar and go back to our base houses for food, ammo, and water cans. Between the front line of cellars and the area back near our Battalion CP there was a small stream about fifteen feet wide. There was a wooden footbridge, about three feet wide, that crossed it. We had to go up two steps to get on the bridge and then go down two steps on the other side.

The Germans had their machine guns aimed right at the footbridge, and you were never sure when they would shoot. At night they would shoot in the dark if they heard a noise.

Larry Choiniere, from our squad, and I were squishing back across the yards and just got to the bridge one night when suddenly "POOOFF!" a flare lit up the whole area as if it were daylight. We had been trained to freeze or stand perfectly still when a flare went off as the German gunners would fire at motion.

This may be easy to do in basic training, but here in real combat it had to be training instinct that took over. I was right at the edge of the bridge and I froze standing there like a tree fully expecting to be cut down by hot lead if I moved. What went through my mind was, "I hope Larry was trained to freeze too, because if he moves we both get it." He was probably thinking the same thing about me as he was only a few steps behind me, and I could hear his muffled voice, "Burn out you S.O.B."

After what seemed like an eternity, darkness fell over us again. The buddy system paid off. We each took care of the other. If one guy had not followed his trained way of defense, both could have been casualties. We waited a few more minutes to make sure the Germans didn't fire a second flare and catch us up on the bridge.

Some of the rooms and cellars on L street were connected, some by a hole in the wall, some by a door frame, and some by a missing wall due to artillery fire. We had to make sure the Germans did not infiltrate the cellar by crawling through one of these interconnecting holes.

One dark night, after I had come up with supplies from the base house, I was soaked through to the skin from pouring rain. I crawled into one of the cellar rooms and lay prone on a big pile of coal briquets. It must have been a huge coal cellar for an apartment building. I lay there shivering for awhile trying not to make any noise. At least I was in out of the rain.

About an hour later I heard movement on the other side of the coal pile. Another man was in the same cellar room. I could not be sure if he had been there when I arrived or if I had dozed off and he came in then. I tried not to even breathe as I strained to hear any telltale noise that might indicate he was a German or American.

He also became as motionless as possible as he, no doubt, strained to hear who I was. We had all become tuned to certain telltale equipment sounds that could give you away. For example, an American mess kit made an identifiable sound. Our GI-issue eating utensils were separate pieces and, unless wrapped in a towel or cloth, could make noise. The German spoon, fork, and knife fit into a spring clip that helped to keep them noiseless and easier to carry.

I had long ago gotten rid of my mess kit fork and knife and only kept the big GI spoon in my shirt pocket. This is the sort of thing one learns in combat that is not taught in training.

As we both lay there, trying to be as quiet as possible, I became aware of how hungry I was. Not having a K-ration in my jacket pocket, I remembered I had a small Milky Way candy bar inside my shirt pocket that I had saved. Ever so slowly, I slid it out of my shirt pocket. It was wet and wrinkled from being crushed against my side when I crawled into the cellar.

Hunger won out over caution as I slowly started to tear off the wrapper. It seemed to me that each tear of the paper wrapper sounded like a drum beat, or was that my heartbeat? As I peeled the paper off the candy bar, I had a mental flashback to that Saturday night at the theater in Nashville when we tore the paper wrappings from the apple pies. Then we only had to be concerned about dirty looks.

After many minutes of careful effort, I placed the candy in my mouth and began to chew. Just then it hit me! "You dope! You are being so careful not to make noise and alert the other man that you forgot about smell! The smell of chocolate being eaten! Now you have done it for sure! If he is German, he will know I am an American because the Germans don't ever have any chocolate."

I swallowed the last bit of that Milky Way and lay there not making a sound, fully expecting a potato masher grenade to land near me in the dark. That night seemed to last an eternity before a dim bluish gray dawn sent some rays down the cellar steps. After it got a little brighter, I carefully moved around the coal pile to the other side.

The other man was gone. I could see the trail of coal briquets that were scattered as he left and there, lying on the pile of briquets, was a German potato masher grenade. In the darkness it could easily be confused with the feel of a briquet. Had the German placed the potato masher on the coal pile and then not been able to find it again in the dark? The chocolate smell would surely have given me away as American, or did he have a cold and couldn't smell? Why didn't he throw that grenade across the pile of coal? I'll never know.

One day back at our base house cellar, we were all grousing about eating K-rations. Praisie "Sam" Harper was from the Florida Everglades. He said, "If you guys can find me some ingredients I can bake some corn bread." So Bill Toll, from Flint, Michigan, and I rooted through the abandoned houses to find boxes of cooking ingredients. We brought them back to Sam who had found some pots and pans and got a fire going in an old oven. Later on we all gathered around the oven and, to a chorus of oohs and aahs, we watched Sam remove a pan of cornbread all steaming hot. We were as excited as little kids at a birthday party, and Sam was as proud as a peacock as we sliced up the cornbread and ate it. It was a feast! There in that dirty, smelly, damp German cellar, we had a taste of home cooking.

The next day, having somehow heard about Sam's cornbread, "Doc," a GI from our 3rd Battalion patrol group, volunteered to go with me across the main bridge to the city where there were more houses we could hunt through for ingredients for Sam's baking. I was so intent on getting the goods for baking that I forgot about the danger of crossing the main bridge on foot instead of racing across in a jeep or truck. Doc said, "I'll go wherever you go. If you aren't afraid, then neither am I."

So we were walking along right out in the open and crossed the bridge and were slowly walking along the approach road when the Germans opened up. Machine gun bullets spattered the puddles right behind us. I said something to Doc about how "that guy forgot to lead a moving target." Doc gave me a look like "boy this guy is a cool customer." But I wasn't really. Ulp!

We ransacked some houses and, with our arms full of small boxes from German kitchens, we smartened up and got a ride back on a truck that was crossing the bridge. That night Sam mixed up the stuff we brought and announced that we would soon have chocolate cake!

The cake came out of the oven sort of flat (not enough yeast I guess), and we dug in and ate it. It had a taste of chocolate, but it was as heavy as lead. No one said much, but we never tried to bake a cake after that.

We were in the same location long enough that we numbered each of the cellars. Like L-22 or L-21 meant house no. 22 in L Company area. One day I was in L-22 when a call came in from 3rd Battalion CP for me to report back to 104th Regiment headquarters for a dental appointment! Imagine! A dental appointment! I said, "I'm not having any teeth problems. Why me?"

"Knock it off, Private. Just get yourself back to the regiment."

Man alive! I have to risk my life running through the rain and over that footbridge and over the main bridge back to the center part of the city just because my name came up on a chart?

When I found my way back and located the dentist he acted so bored. This whole war offended him. He complained about the poor facilities he had to use as he probed my mouth. If only he could come up front with us for an overnight visit he would get his eyes opened.

"Who gives these dentists such control over our lives?" I wondered. I remember the day on Normandy when I was told to report to a dentist out in an open field. He had a tripod folding dental chair, nothing but natural daylight, and a pedal-operated drill that he used to drill out a filling he didn't like. "Some dental care," I thought. If your name is on his Come Up File, you report to his chair even if you are leading an attack.

He fooled around so much that it began to get dark. I said that I had to get back to my cellar, could he please hurry up?

"How important is your job up there anyhow?" he asked in an annoyed tone.

I said, "I have to get back before dark." I figured there was no use trying to explain to this guy. Eventually he turned me loose and I legged it all the way back to L-22.

The next day we were sitting on the dirt floor of L-22 cellar with only light from one small candle when the field phone rang. An L Company sergeant answered and said, "OK, I got it," and hung up. "Of all things, now I've got to go out in the rain and find some guy named Courtney," he said.

"Hey, that's me!" I said.

"You Courtney?"

"Yeah."

"Well you are supposed to report back right now to Peter 1. (Peter 1 was a code name for 3rd Battalion CP.) You are to go on pass to Metz," he said.

At once a hue and cry went up from about twenty GIs from L Company. "How does a guy get a pass? Who do you know?" And so forth.

I replied, "Hey guys, I'm an old man in the YD. I came over with the outfit," trying to justify that I deserved a pass. Most of the L Company men and the antitank men up there had come over as replacements.

This time I threw caution to the wind as I raced back over the footbridge and ran to my base house cellar. "Hey Chapo!" I yelled to Frank Chapo of our squad. "You go up to L-22 and replace me, cause I'm going to Metz on pass."

Frank started putting on his gear to go when he let out a loud deep cough. He had another deep cold. I said, "Hold up Frank. You can't go. Your cough would give away our position at night. Kanelos, you get your gear on and go. Take some food with you for our squad."

Outside I gave John Kanelos some directions how to find L-22 and how to cross the footbridge, and so forth. Then I started to run toward the Battalion CP pillbox. I was slipping on the mudcovered cobblestones as I approached the CP, and a 2^1/$_2$-ton truck was just starting to pull away. The guys on the truck yelled, "Courtney. Come on. We gave up on you. We waited long enough!" I ran to the rear of the truck as it was gaining speed. I held up my arms, and they pulled me over the tailgate and onto the floor of the truck. I came that close to missing an overnight pass.

About a dozen of us from the 3rd Battalion rode through the late afternoon rain until we arrived in Metz. Wow! What a sight! A city with lights on! Our first time on the Continent to see lights at night.

Our second big thrill was to realize that we were far enough behind the front not to have to worry about artillery or mortar fire. What a free feeling. We really felt alive! It was great!

We were put up in a big five-story building called the Yankee Hotel, which formerly was used as Gestapo Headquarters. There were rows of cots for sleeping and real showers. On the third floor there was a real water closet toilet.

That night we were served supper seated at tables like a real restaurant. We laughed and joked and said, "Please pass the salt, sir," just like high-class people instead of K-ration dogfaces.

"Red" Hubert from Pittsburgh was one of the guys from our platoon who came on the same truck I did. We went into town and drank some beer and wine. Red headed back to the YD Hotel because he was eager to try out the real toilet on the third floor.

I went to see the big Cathedral of Metz, which I had only seen from the outside when our division was here before. It is huge and very impressive. Built around 1200, I was told. Someone forgot to put in pews and kneelers, I thought, until I learned that the big churches in Europe don't have any.

Although the city of Metz was trying to get back to normal, it was hard to do since every one of the arched stone bridges had been blown up by the Germans before they surrendered the city.

Americans had put in some big wooden footbridges to cross the river, but no vehicles could cross. I often wondered how long after the war it took the French to restore all those bridges.

All too soon, our 48-hour pass ended, and we climbed onto the trucks to head back to our outfit. To our surprise, we did not go back to the rubble and street fighting of Saarlautern. We learned that our regiment had been relieved by units of the 65th Infantry Division, which had just arrived from the States. Instead we arrived in the quaint little French village of Hargarten and were billeted in little houses that had seen no destruction.

When I got back to my squad, I learned that Kanelos, the man who went up to L-22 in my place, had been killed. It seems that the night Kanelos got up to the cellar, it began to rain fairly hard, a cold rain with cold wind. The man who was assigned to go around to the street side of the building after dark to watch for German patrols decided it was too wet and too cold so he stayed at the back side of the building in a doorway out of the rain.

The Germans came across the narrow street and placed a satchel charge (bag full of dynamite) against the cellar wall, ran a wire back to their side of the street, and pushed the plunger down to explode the charge. The whole building exploded, and the stone and mortar fell into the cellar of L-22, crushing the life out of 18 men including Cpl. John Kanelos of Chicago.

John's father owned a candy company named Joy Candy of Chicago. About six weeks later, he sent our platoon a letter about John and his thanks to us for being his friends. He also sent us a box of Joy Candy.

I always remembered the 48-hour pass to Metz that saved my life. Frank Chapo said he will always remember the heavy cough that probably saved his.

6

Across the Rhine
and
the Race to Berlin

HARGARTEN WAS A PLEASANT LITTLE VILLAGE with most of its quaint little houses intact. Each squad had a house to itself, as we moved in with the French families.

Across the road from our house, there was a young French girl named Teresa who had learned to speak English in school. She was very happy to have Americans to talk to and we all got along fine.

We got the word that we could now become the 26th Division again, and the blue and olive drab shoulder patches were issued to each man. No one bothered to inform us whether the disappearance of the YD had confused the Germans or not.

Anyhow, we were glad to rip off the 95th Division patches and once more wear our own 26th Division patch. Bless her heart, young Teresa offered to sew our YDs on our shirts and field jackets, and we were quick to accept her offer. She did a very neat job too. We all felt better to regain our identity as the YD.

About the same time, guys came around with stencils and relettered our vehicle bumpers with 26 DIV and 3BN 104RGT.

By now most of our jeeps had a steel bar, usually a metal fence post, welded straight up on the front bumper with the top 12 inches bent toward the front. This may not have looked very military, but it saved lives. Back in Alsace-Lorraine, we learned that retreating Germans left many killer mines and booby traps behind. One of the most insidious was a piano wire, very thin and very strong, strung across the

road and tied from one tree to another on the other side just at the
height to hit the driver or passenger in the throat. A good many soldiers lost their heads as they raced down the road in attack and suddenly ZZZITT! It was an awful way to die. The welded bar, like an
upside down L, would hit the wire and snap it in two before the wire
could do any damage.

Another mean trap was called a "shoe mine." It was a mine en-
cased in a wooden box and planted in the soil. Since it did not have a
metal casing, it could not be discovered by a metal detector and therefore caused a lot of casualties. It was not explosive enough to kill a
man, but just enough to blow off a foot and put him out of action.
After one attack across a field, we found a GI boot with a foot still
inside. There was virtually no defense against the shoe mine.

After several days of rest in Hargarten, the GIs, maybe to release
tension from the horrible conditions of street warfare in the cellars of
Saarlautern, loosened up and became little boys again. No one can
understand this unless he has lived through it. Tough guys from just a
few days ago now sat around a table and played cards. No, not just
poker, but Old Maid and Thank You for Your Bundle. I even remember a tough sergeant playing Fish with Teresa. "Give me all your sev-
ens!" Hard to imagine.

No one talked about what we had been through, but most of the
conversation was about boyhood back home. One guy recounted how
he won the marbles championship back in Brattlesboro, Massachusetts. Hardened veteran troopers became kids once more, and no one
felt ashamed. Everyone seemed to laugh and enjoy it.

Quickly the news was passed that a Red Cross Donut Wagon had
arrived in town, and we all rushed down to find it. Wow! It was really
here with real American girls speaking English! "Hi ya soldier, how do
you want your coffee?"

We all jammed up close to the enclosed van where the girls passed
coffee and donuts through big side windows. I think the windows and
the counters were designed not only to serve the coffee and donuts
but to protect the Red Cross girls from being crushed by the enthusiastic GIs. I went back to the window again and again for coffee and
donuts until I got sick to my stomach.

One who has ever been in a foreign country for a long time can
appreciate our happiness as we heard the girls speak English. American
English too! We hung on every word they said as if it was something
that once lost would never return. Those Red Cross girls handed out

coffee and donuts, but they handed out more than that. They told us with their smiles that we were not forgotten and that people appreciated what we were doing.

When we wrote letters home, we all told our families how much we appreciated those volunteers from the States who came over to cheer us up. It did not happen that often, but when it did we were grateful. It was a touch of home.

We moved to a relatively quiet sector near Falck, dug in, and spent most of our time observing a lightly held front. Before dawn, for several days, Larry Choiniere and I plus two FOs (forward observers for artillery) were taken by jeep to man an outpost overlooking a valley to our front. We were there to give the alarm if the Germans attacked.

Larry and I stayed in a well-built log bunker formerly occupied by the Germans. The two FOs were about one hundred yards from us in another log bunker, and we had a phone line strung between the two bunkers. Larry and I would take two-hour turns manning a .50 caliber machine gun pointing down the valley while the other guy stayed in the bunker.

We did not have a watch to tell us the time since the watch I liberated from a German soldier at Buderscheid had been smashed somewhere along the line. Time dragged along all day as we sat there motionless. The two GIs manning the FO bunker had a watch, so we would whistle over the phone to get their attention, and then they would tell us the time so we could change places. One afternoon I whistled and whistled, but no answer came. I thought those guys must have been goofing off or asleep. Later on I heard a whistle on the phone. When I picked it up, the guy told me his buddy had been killed by a sniper. Even on a quiet front men still die.

After our solitary sentry duty, Larry and I came back to our platoon to learn that there was a small USO show in the village. We hurried to join the company in this small building and to see some song and dance acts. We were just getting warmed up to the show when the lead girl singer collapsed on the stage. They carried her off stage, and a man came up to the microphone and soberly asked, "Is there a doctor in the house?" All of the GIs roared laughing as we thought it was all part of the act. The man said, "I am serious, we need a doctor! Sally is really bad off!"

A concerned hush, sort of an embarrassed silence, fell over the crowd. Our battalion medics hurried forward and disappeared behind the stage curtain. Then the Master of Ceremonies came to the mike and explained that they were traveling from outfit to outfit and giving several shows each day and they were tired and worn out. Sally was so exhausted that they begged her not to go on, but she insisted that if the soldiers could keep going she could too. So she went on stage to perform and passed out.

The show ended then and we all quietly left the building. Most of us were commenting on the courage of Sally the performer. She was a real trooper.

We were back in our foxholes when the mail caught up with us. From the letters we learned that the folks back home think, now that the Bulge is over, the war will soon be over. Trouble is, the German troops don't believe this. We still have a long way to go, and we wonder how many of us will still be around when it ends.

I was sitting in my hole writing a letter home when to my surprise Duquette, our driver from Fall River, Massachusetts, rode up on an old nag of a horse. We all laughed and yelled "Hi Yo Silver" as Duke clomped around riding bareback on this awful-looking horse that he found just wandering around.

We moved to an assembly point near Teterchen to get ready for a "jump off" attack.

The next day the attack went so well that we got strung out along a moving front, and some of us were posted along the road to show the way to other elements coming up behind us. I was standing there with my carbine in my hands when a Polish slave laborer who had been liberated came along and greeted me with "*Dzien Dobry*" (good day). He gave me a bottle of wine that he was carrying and by words and gestures made me understand that this was his thanks for being freed by Americans. He was a thin, hungry looking man who looked older than his years, but his eyes shone with excitement at being released from his Nazi guards. I still can see his big toothy grin. "America! Gud!" he kept saying as he passed out of sight heading away from the Germans.

When I got picked up by our squad truck, I passed the bottle around and it was soon emptied. One of the guys said, "Bet you can't hit that tree, Bazooka!" (Bazooka was my nickname at the time) and he pointed to a tree we were passing. I threw the bottle! Smash! I hit the tree and the guys cheered! The Polish man would have been proud.

At Holtzmühle we recrossed the border into France and moved through Bous and Ensdorf. Here we saw the most beautiful sunset. It looked just as it does back home. I wondered what the folks at home were doing at that moment.

Our advance was slowed up by a herd of cows that somehow had gotten the right of way as they headed for the barn. There was a tank stopped right near us, and I started joking with the GI in the turret.

He said he was 1A and had been drafted, and I said I had enlisted, my two brothers had been drafted, but now my brother John who was hurt in Texas had been sent home and classified as 1CAH. Another tanker stuck his head up out of the hatch and said, "What is 1CAH? I never heard of that classification."

I said, "1CAH stands for one Courtney at home!" and all the guys laughed as the column moved forward again.

That night we arrived in Remeling and moved in with French civilians. I remember how I bargained with a grizzled old woman for some eggs. She was definitely not happy to have Americans staying in her house.

In the back of the house was a still. An old Frenchman was puttering around it, and I picked up a tall, thin measuring glass and started to draw off a drink from the barrel. The old man protested and spoke so rapidly that my French could not keep up. I decided he was just mad that I was taking a drink. We had some new replacements in our squad, and I was showing off how we handle civilians, so I ignored the old man and started to drink the schnapps. Wow! I thought my helmet had wrinkled! My eyes smarted and saw a flash of light, so I stopped drinking.

Just then Alfred Duquette, who could speak fluent French, came into the back room, and the old man excitedly talked to him. Then Duke told me that the old man was trying to tell me that the batch was not cooked yet, and I had been drinking almost pure alcohol! I looked around kind of sheepishly and left the barn.

The next morning it was very cold as dawn broke, and we all got a kick out of watching the townspeople assemble at the pump for water. Apparently this was a daily ritual. What amused us was how the men gathered together to talk over events while the women pumped the water, filled their jugs, and carried them home. Rural French etiquette.

Jake Lipps, who had taken over as squad leader in the Bulge when Vic Martin was hit, was trimming his huge mustache with a pair of scissors he had found in the house we were in. He used to kid me a lot and said, "Bazooka! You found a home in the Army."

"Not me," I was protesting when Lieutenant Deviese came in the door. In combat we no longer jumped to attention as we had to do in the States. We just greeted him with "Hi, Lieutenant!"

"Well, Lipps, are you ready for another campaign?" he said. We all thought to ourselves, "Another campaign? Don't we ever rest? Is this to keep up forever? Are we the only division in the ETO?"

Then we took it as all infantrymen usually learn to take things. Well, if we must, we must. I guess someone has to win this war. Why did I have to get into the infantry anyway? I wonder how many of us will survive this one?

So we took Saarburg. We are back in Germany again and this time we are here to stay. We thought that when we run out of German towns to take the war will be over. Well, that was something to look forward to anyhow.

It was the rainy season now and we were all wearing either a raincoat or a poncho. Each man was equipped with a heavy, water-repellent raincoat. These long coats came to your knees and were so rubberized that you would really sweat if you had to wear one for very long. The coats did not breathe.

I remember when we were in the old World War I trench area of the Argonne Forest that we were issued the new ponchos. These had no pockets or buttons. They were one piece with a hole for your head to go through and an attached hood.

The advantage of the poncho was that it could protect you from the rain and also keep your weapon dry, since it covered your rifle too. Another advantage I found when I was carrying an M-1 carbine was that I could sling my rifle upside down with the barrel pointing downward. As it hung free on my shoulder under the loose-hanging poncho, I could slap the barrel with my hand and the rifle would flip quickly into firing position in my hands. We used to say we could "quick draw" like the Western cowboys.

The disadvantage of the poncho was that your knees got soaked because the poncho was not long enough to cover them. In later years the Army made the poncho longer to correct this.

It was pouring rain as we came through the woods at Ackfem, and we found a lot of equipment abandoned by the Germans. It was quite a mess. Next we moved on to Irsch, where we lived in a German hospital and stayed there a few days while armor support assembled around us for a big drive. We saw some movies and for the first time saw some fairly new ones. I remember how we all enjoyed the *Keys to the Kingdom* with Gregory Peck as a priest in China. It was a very sweet movie.

We waited and wondered and then it came, the jump off. When we entered Brittain, we saw what devastation our artillery could do. The next town we took was Hausbach, and we saw evidence that the Germans had left in a hurry. This was a good sign.

Rimlingen was like a ghost town as all the Germans had moved east with their retreating army. Here we looted eggs, and they tasted good as we cooked them on German frying pans. We were giving the Germans a taste of what they had been doing to others for years.

In Remsbach we came upon streams of Russian, French, Polish, and Italian ex-POWs who clogged the roads. How happy they all were to see us, and I'll never forget the cheers of *"Gud Americanski!" "Vive L'Amérique!"* It gave one a real feeling of satisfaction that we had liberated these poor people.

At Aussen we were able to leave dirt roads and go on a smooth, paved highway. Now there was something new to us old mudders—dust! We became a fearful sight as we were covered with dust all over, clothes, face, and all.

Entering Hummelbach, we caught up with fleeing German civilians who were pushing funny-looking horse carts with their possessions on board. Their first sight of Americans were these dirty, dusty YDs who looked like wild men. We didn't receive any pleasant looks from these people. We were no longer the "conquering heroes" or "liberators."

As we moved past Aschbach we saw two of the famed Luftwaffe planes lying crumpled in the dirt where they had fallen after an encounter with the United States Army Air Force.

At Dirmingen we all grinned when we saw same Russian slave workers who had commandeered a German truck and were heading for our rear. They didn't have any idea where they were going, just that they were going in the opposite direction from the dreaded Nazis.

We stopped overnight in a schoolhouse at Neiderlinxweiler where we saw large pictures of *der Führer* hanging on the wall. We leafed through the textbooks to see lots of pictures of Goebbels, Goering, and so forth. Some education!

In one day we took Donzweiler, Lautrenbach, Spesbach, and Ramstein. Here Frank Chapo picked up a huge swastika flag, and I got a German officer's cap as a souvenir. Jake was complaining that we were getting too much junk on the truck. We found warehouses with candy bars and bottles of brandy. After we tasted them we did not like either one, so we stood on the road and passed them out to other GI vehicles. No one came back for seconds!

At Landstuhl our whole company moved into a large building, and I remember that I had a bad cold so I drank a whole bottle of cognac. Sergeant McKittrick left me off guard duty that night so I could kill the cold.

The next morning the cold was gone, but I felt miserable. I did not even want to look at food. Here some of our squad came back with jars of cherries and bottles of cream. They were having a feast and kept yelling to me, "Hey Courtney! Have some cherries and cream! They are great!" I couldn't even look. What a time to find such food.

We found some eggs and were cooking them over outdoor fires in the street while the 10th Armored Division assembled more armor for the next breakthrough.

Nearby there was a large truck and trailer filled with the household furnishings of a wealthy Nazi party member. We watched the German people loot their own as they emptied the trailer. The German nation was cracking fast.

We read in the *Stars and Stripes* how our other armies were on the move, and we realized, as did the Germans, that this was the beginning of the end. We wondered what the crossing of the Rhine would be like, as we remembered our crossings of the Moselle, the Sûre, and the Saar.

At Kindsbach, along the roads we saw trucks and tanks littered everywhere. They were filled with dead German soldiers in grotesque postures just as the bullets of the .50 caliber machine guns of our P-47 Thunderbolts had caught them. From German POWs we learned that they hated and feared our P-47s, which they called *Jabos* (fighter-bombers). They told us how German soldiers would be killed in their foxholes by the armor-piercing bullets of the P-47s, which would smash right through the ground and into their bunkers.

We pushed our way through a forest and came down a hill and entered Kaiserslautern on a destroyed railroad track. The Germans' camouflage was to no avail as our Air Force used saturation bombing techniques and didn't miss a building. There were railroad tracks twisted like Philadelphia pretzels and steam engines standing straight up in the air on their noses! Later we saw pictures of this in American magazines and the pictures were not exaggerated.

The sun came out as we approached Dansenberg, and along the road we met a group of Russian and French escapees who had stopped to rest. I stood up on the load of ammo on our truck and put on a black top hat I had acquired and gave them some impersonations. Then I put on the German officers dress cap and with my black comb held under my nose I did one of Adolf Hitler. You should have heard them scream with laughter!

I shouted, "Hitler wants peace! Just a piece of Austria and a piece of Poland and a piece of Russia." Those guys really got the joke and laughed uproariously. We shared our chocolate and cigarettes with them. You should have seen the grateful look in their eyes. We all felt pretty good that day.

Waldlelnengen was well named as all we could see was dense woods. Then we arrived in Elmstein where I remember a young girl of about eighteen who could speak fluent English. She tried her best to explain to us how good Hitler was and that all he wanted was to have more living space for the German people and raw materials for their industry. Poor propaganda-fed child, I thought. What will we do with such warped minds? It will be quite a problem.

We went through Appenthal with no opposition because the terrain was so level and open that the Germans did not attempt any defense. In Esthal we began to have *Volkssturm* opposition. Sometimes it was serious, sometimes comical.

Volkssturm means People's Army. It was Hitler's desperate idea to call up all the men of any age to form a militia to fight the invading Americans. To qualify them as "soldiers," they were given a red and black armband to wear on their left arm that had *Volkssturm* printed on it. Some men wore their military caps saved from World War I. Mostly members of the *Volkssturm* were older men and young boys and sometimes young teenage girls.

At Frankeneck we killed a big gobbler turkey and put it in an oven as we expected to be here for the night. We had only cooked him for about half an hour when we got orders to move. We put the roasting pan with the turkey inside on the truck. Later on we ended up in Neidenfels. We got into a house, started a fire in the oven, and started to cook him again.

Move again! Grab the turkey pan and go. This time we dug in in an open field and tried to cook our gobbler over the coals of an open fire. When a Messerschmitt night fighter buzzed low over us in a strafing attack, we hurriedly covered up the glowing embers.

Now it was dark, and we moved again to Frankenstein where we felt sure we would stay the night. Sam Harper basted the turkey in the new oven and the smell was great. We all were looking forward to a late turkey supper when Sergeant Piquette came to our house and told us to load up. We were going to be the first unit of our 3rd Battalion to cross the Rhine River that night. That was too much! We took the old gobbler out of the oven, tore him apart with our bare hands, and ate him half raw. It sure tasted good, and we were glad to be rid of our white elephant.

Our caravan pulled out of the town and moved swiftly along a stone-paved roadway. In the darkness we came to a Y in the road where the lead vehicle took the right fork, and Duke, our driver, did not see it make the turn and we took the left fork.

We raced along in the dark trying to catch up to the column, not knowing that it had gone the other way. Finally we realized that we were lost. We got into Munchweiler and hooked up with a TD (tank destroyer) outfit where we spent the rest of the night.

From a hilltop we could see much Ack-Ack (antiaircraft artillery) and red tracer shells in the air over the Rhine. We could see and hear fighter dogfights over the area. It looked like a Fourth of July celebration back home.

The next morning we heard about all the activity over the bridge that night. We wondered if the rest of our outfit got safely across the pontoon bridge. We kidded Duke about losing our way, but we all thought maybe it was a blessing in disguise after we saw the German fighters attacking the bridge.

We had joined the 691st TDs to make our way to the Rhine. It was my brother John's old outfit from Texas. Most of the guys knew John and told me to say hello to him in my next letter. They said to tell John that the Chief got it. Chief was a nickname they had given to a Cherokee man who was in the 691st. I remember John telling me about some wild times they had with the Chief.

As we passed through Stenbuhl, we saw an American MP making a group of German civilians take down a log roadblock. The MP seemed to be enjoying himself doing it. We noticed a very well dressed German who was doing more watching than working. We called this to the attention of the MP, and he quickly prodded the man to work. It was good to see these people handed some of their own medicine.

At Dreisen we got directions to the bridge. As we rolled through Bolendorf, we passed a whole tank column headed for the Rhine. I hoped the pontoons were strong enough to hold all that weight. The Shermans got rolling so fast that at a turn in the paved road I saw one tank spin completely around. We thought we were in a pretty big army when we saw all this armor. We wondered where it all was when were back in those holes in Luxembourg.

The road traffic was exciting as we got closer to the bridge approach. It reminded me of Race Street in Philadelphia and the approach to the Delaware River bridge.

Our column pulled into a big field assembly area in sight of the river. GIs came to each truck, jeep, TD, or tank and told the crew to check for gasoline. If your engine died for any reason on the bridge, your vehicle would be pushed over the side into the river. Nothing must slow or stop the column on the bridge.

Always the scrounger, I was able to bum a slice of bread and to fill my canteen cup with coffee from an Engineer kitchen tent nearby. I just made it back to the truck when it was our turn to go across.

We were all excited like kids at an amusement park. Here we go! Ca-Lunk! Ca-Lunk! Blunk! Glunk! We were up and on the bridge in an endless column of trucks and tanks. Hundreds of canvas and rubber boats had been lashed together to form a bridge. On top of this was a double track made of steel girders laid end to end. Each driver fit his wheels into the two grooves and tried to hold 'er steady. I don't know what we expected. We had pointed for the Rhine for so long and here it was. It was just another muddy river, but a big one.

After all the activity the night before, we expected to be bombed and strafed as we crossed. Not a shot was fired. No German planes were in sight and we were glad to see the P-47s with their red noses flying over us. It was 1415 hours on March 25, 1945, on the pontoon bridge that made history. I yelled to all the guys around us in the columns, "Just for the history book record, remember that Pfc. Courtney was drinking coffee as we crossed the Rhine."

On the eastern side of the bridge, we went through Nierstein, which was a completely burned out town. At Geinsheim we stayed overnight and watched a fierce aerial duel over the Rhine. Our Ack-Ack boys put up so much shellfire that it lit up the sky like daylight, and we saw several enemy planes go down in bright red flames.

When dawn broke the pontoon bridge was still there and armor kept pouring across. Where did we get all those tanks?

We moved to Leeheim and saw plenty of nice homes in this area that weren't even touched by shellfire. It seemed that since the Germans were in their homeland now they are retreating to save their homes from destruction. It was O.K. with us as long as they kept retreating.

Near Wolfskelen we were slowed up by lines of refugees along the route heading west. I remember an old Polish woman plodding along the road with all that remained of her worldly goods in a huge bag on her back. She was dressed all in black like most of the grandmothers seemed to be. She looked so exhausted that she might pass out at any moment.

I motioned to her to stop and sit down on a nearby tree stump, which she did after dropping her heavy bag with a thump. I opened a C-ration can and gave her the round saltine crackers and pieces of hard candy. Then I filled the C-ration can with water from my canteen.

She smiled at me gratefully as she chewed on the crackers and drank the water. "*Dzienkuna*," she said in Polish, which I later learned means thank you. We had to move on, and I waved good-bye to her as she sat on the stump. Scenes like this make war hard to understand. I remembered a verse of scripture, "a cup of cold water given in my name . . ."

At Goddelau we were in the railroad station and had fun issuing each other tickets to Berlin. We looked over the railroad yards and noted the differences between German and American railroads. Since I grew up in the railroad town of Altoona, home of the Pennsylvania Railroad, I was viewed as the expert in our discussion of trains. We all noted how much smaller the German boxcars were than the American models. Their steam engine whistles had a shriller, more piercing sound than ours.

We assembled in the Phillips Hospital area near Crumstadt for our armor support to assemble. By now our drive was gaining momentum and we felt that there was nothing that could stop us.

We started to roll through Eschollbrucken, Pfungstadt, and Eberstadt. German resistance now was sporadic. They would retreat through town after town and then suddenly turn around and put up a fight. Some towns were starting to put up white flags hoping to spare themselves from damage.

We used to say it was like going to work. We no longer dug a foxhole every time we stopped as we stayed in houses or barns. Each morning we would eat our breakfast of whatever German food we could find, usually *eier* (eggs) and brown bread. Then we would load on the trucks and tanks and start chasing Germans. The line company GIs rode on the tanks and some rode on our 1¹/₂-ton trucks with our AT platoon.

Old Sergeant Farren from K Company used to be hoisted up to sit on the front of a Sherman. The story was that he never got over all of his buddies who were killed in Luxembourg, and he drank heavily every night to try to blot out his memories. The newer replacements were taking care of him.

Then there was Sergeant Miller from L Company. He used to ask if he could have his squad ride on our truck because we joked a lot together. He was a real character. I remember that he hated to wear a steel helmet, so he would always manage to lose his. One day as we prepared to attack a town, our battalion surgeon saw him without a helmet. He generously insisted that Miller take his helmet so Miller reluctantly did.

Later in the day, as we moved out of that town, Miller trudged past the captain surgeon with no helmet on his head. Miller looked kind of sheepish, but neither he nor the captain said a word.

We were really living off the land now. We ate whatever we could find in German pantries. Mostly eggs, chickens, jarred fruit, and hard round wheels of black or brown bread that you needed a sharp knife or bayonet to cut. Joe Sorrentino and his kitchen must be far behind us, but we did not miss him now.

Our trucks and jeeps all carried Nazi flags and all sorts of souvenirs. A favorite trick was to take down a street sign reading Adolf Hitler Platz and fasten it to the hood of a jeep. One day we had a large picture of Adolf on our radiator, but we decided we didn't like it there so we tacked it up on a fence and threw our trench knives at it. Some old German women in town were shocked and kept shouting at us like offended schoolteachers that we would get into big trouble for making fun of *der Führer*. Evidently they did not realize that Hitler could not do anything about it.

At Rossdorf I found a woman's black fur hat, and when I wore it I looked just like a Russian cossack. I put on quite a show for the boys until I was told not to wear it anymore but to put on my helmet. Guess one Miller per division is enough. I gave the hat to Larry Choiniere to wear under his helmet as he had lost his wool knit cap. It really made him look like an old woman.

By now, being in Germany was no longer a novelty. We were quite sick of hearing from the "poor German" people their sad tales of how they were mistreated. They expected us to believe them.

We used to laugh at them and sing *"Deutschland über Alles, zwei Kartoffeln das ist Alles."* This was a parody of the German national anthem, "Germany over All," to which we added "two potatoes, that's all." This would really make the German civilians mad.

At Dieburg all the houses in town carried white sheets. I laughed at the irony of it as I noticed that the white sheets hung from the same poles from which the swastikas had formerly hung.

In Babenhausen we were told that we had moved so fast that our division right flank was exposed. We were to keep a sharp lookout for German armor. We moved out in the field next to town and dug in for the first time in weeks. We saw plenty of tanks the next day, but the 10th Armored Division came up and took care of them. Here we joined up with our buddies from the 4th Armored. A colonel of the 4th Armored Division came up to our gun position and asked if we were men of the YD. When we said yes, he said, "That is a crack outfit. We always feel pretty safe when you guys are around."

At Zellhausen we found plenty of German jeeps and civilian cars, all out of gas and abandoned. Sgt. Doug Beck, our platoon artist, painted big white stars on the door of the cars as we thought we would ride in them. However, we soon got the order to "let 'em be."

We stopped long enough at Seligenstadt to get new uniforms issued. Now if we could only get a shower. We still looked and smelled like a mess.

The mail sure was slow catching up with us on this drive. We longed for the day when it would arrive. A soldier in combat lives for mail from home. I used to laugh to myself that my mother would take up the first page of her letters giving me the weather report for Altoona, which arrived in Europe six weeks later! However, I enjoyed seeing her handwriting on the pages. She always assured me that she was praying for me and so was my old friend Katie O'Keefe who was a parish housekeeper back home.

At Alzenau the village was bypassed by the column, and Pinky told us our platoon was assigned to flush it out. We moved from house to house looking for any resistance. One door was locked, so I backed off across the room, gave a run, and lunged against the door with my .45 pistol in my hand.

I blasted the door off the hinges and crashed into a room and came face to face with a thoroughly frightened young woman seated in a rocker and nursing her baby. I excused myself and moved on.

We took Glenhausen and got sick eating eggs. It was my fault. In a darkened pantry I grabbed a jar of grease for the pan and cooked the eggs. We couldn't figure out why there was so much bluish smoke in the kitchen and it turned out that I had grabbed a jar of homemade soap, not grease. UGH!

At Marborn we got mail! Wow! Three letters and a copy of the *Stars and Stripes*! One of the letters from my brother told me that by the time I got the letter the war in Europe would be over. Hot dog, I thought, should I forward this letter to Uncle Adolf?

At Steinau I found some very good pipes and I selected one and gave the others to our squad. We found a warehouse here full of German cigarettes and handkerchiefs. What a combination. The cigarettes were awful! No wonder the German POWs always asked for an American cigarette.

Jennings A. Martin, from Louisiana, was called JA for short. I remember the day he read out loud a story in the *Stars and Stripes* about the number of French troops who had been killed by land mines in the part of Saarlautern we had been in. It seems the mines did not get set off due to the ground being frozen, but after it thawed, and the French troops moved in, the mines exploded. Probably the French assumed that the mines had been cleared by the Americans when we were there. We all sort of looked at each other after the importance of the story sank in. How many times had we been saved from death? How many times did we have left?

I remember the town of Stork especially because it looked just like travel posters of Europe. It must be nice to visit such places in peace-time.

At Magdlos we found some jarred turkey meat in a cellar and decided to try it out. It proved to be excellent, and we made special efforts to look for more of it in our travels. In Flieden we saw a car that had been run over by a tank. It looked like one of Joe Sorrentino's pancakes. It made us wonder where our company kitchen, was but we now ate better without it.

We were climbing into the mountains around Neustadt, and they looked to me just like the mountains back home in Pennsylvania. I wondered how long it would be until I saw my own mountains again.

At Tiefengruben I remember all the fresh graves that had German crosses on them.

We hit opposition near Zigeal and fired HE (high explosive) rounds into a church steeple that was being used as an observation point. The line companies had to wade across the Fulda River to get into the town. Our squad found a way by driving on railroad tracks about a quarter of a mile and then right through the train station. We chewed up one of the tires on the 57 mm gun on the tracks in the process.

At Johannesburg we stayed in a house with a small German family, and they were terrified. They had been told that the "Amis" killed all civilians. Boy were they surprised when Frank Chapo put a record on their hand-cranked Victrola and played music. They could not believe that we Americans weren't barbarians. It shook them up a bit though when we blasted a Tiger tank not far from their house.

Fulda put up quite a battle. The Germans were well dug in and fought hard. As they retreated, they had work crews of POWs, slave laborers, and local civilians prepare each town with well-concealed fox-holes. They even carried the dirt away so we could not tell a foxhole had been dug nearby. They built strong walls of logs to block entrances to town gates and in larger towns they built concrete pillboxes commanding street intersections. These were ingeniously designed so that you had to hit the machine gun ports precisely. No ricochet rounds would be effective. Some of these were manned, some were not. It depended on how fast our attack hit the town.

The town of Ruckers wasn't much, but the name did remind me of the Ruckers family in Columbia, South Carolina, who were so nice to Ron McGregor and me when they had us visit their home when we were at Fort Jackson.

Next we were moving through the resort section of the country around Rasdorf. I thought of how many rich Americans used to visit here, and now here we were, grimy and dirty, but here for a different purpose. The people were not happy to see this group of tourists arriving. On a huge hill near Bremen (in Hessen) we saw a huge castle, the kind we used to see in storybooks as a child. We wanted to go through it but the war wouldn't wait.

Our squad leader, Jake Lipps, carried a map of Europe, and each time the *Stars and Stripes* would show a map of our gains, Jake would pencil our area in black. We thought about the time when that map would be all black. Sometimes it seemed so far away. Around Neubach and Diedorf we could see more schlosses or castles on the surrounding hillsides. It was a beautiful area. We also saw milk cows being used to pull a wagon, something you would not see in the States.

Meiningen was a real city where we got into the Royal Palace of Prince Royce of the Hapsburgs. I remember a beautiful girl who spoke perfect English as she showed us through. We liberated a large number of Russian POWs here. Sergeant McKittrick gave one big Ukrainian a can of German peaches with a spoon and his eyes lit up with delight as he spooned the peaches into his mouth. Sergeant McKittrick told him it did his heart good to see him eat.

We took a position at the top of a long hill in a house owned by Col. Otto Benken. I know his name because he left a lot of letterhead stationery behind that I used for months in my letters to home. My dad wrote back and said how nice it was of Mr. Benken to give me the stationery. Ha!

Duke, Sam, and Larry went out to hunt for eggs and came back with three German prisoners after a brief firefight. Otto's home was furnished with expensive loot he had taken from all over Europe. It was exquisitely furnished. In his bedroom closet I found a long rubber truncheon he might have used to beat prisoners, a heavy sheepskin paratrooper's coat, and a beautiful officer's dress sword complete with engraved swastikas and a lion's head with ruby eyes. I managed later to ship the sword and coat home where the sword now hangs over a door in our family room.

When we left Meiningen, I liberated Otto's typewriter, which I used to type letters home and also diary notes of our movements and experiences.

The weather turned chilly at night as we headed east, and I wore my paratrooper coat. Some of the guys had found rabbit skin vests which they wore under their combat jackets. One day our surgeon saw them and advised them not to wear the rabbit skins. He said that if they are wounded the rabbit fur will go all through the wound and makes it hard to clean. Typical GIs, they wore them anyway.

At Mabendorf there was a beautiful lake complete with diving boards in the swimming area. It reminded me of Kennywood Park back in Pittsburgh. Another town we all remember is Suhl where there were rows of beautiful homes on a hillside. Russian slave laborers worked the factories there. Many of the GIs got to go through the pistol factory and pick up a souvenir. They were Zeiss cameras, but there was no film to use in them. I was not lucky enough to get a camera.

In the house where our squad stayed, the people spoke fluent English. They were telling us how hard the war was on them although the whole place looked pretty good. While we were talking Larry Choiniere had been scrounging in the cellar. He let out a yell. "Look what I found!" He came up out of the cellar carrying cans of Dole pineapple. He hurriedly opened one and sat down to eat the fruit.

The German family was all flustered and I wondered why until the daughter explained to me that two of the women were relatives from Berlin who had moved here to escape the war. The family never told the relatives about their cache of food in the cellar, and now they were embarrassed. Larry, Frank, and I got a big kick out of it.

One night we sat around a table with a man, a woman, and a young girl. Frank spoke Hungarian to the woman who translated to her husband in Portuguese who spoke to the girl, Hada, in German. What an international conversation that was. They told us of the brutalities of life on the Russian front.

At Hirschbach Robby Robinson and Tex VanNorman had just returned from a pass to Metz. They were sorry they had missed Suhl when the guys showed them their souvenir pistols. We were traveling through the province of Thuringia, which was a much written about part of Germany. There were beautiful views if only we had film for our cameras.

In the villages many of the homes were built close together. They were whitewashed, spanking clean. The roofs were high and extended over the cobblestone street. windows were of many panes of diamond-shaped glass with heavy, wooden shutters. At the second floor windows there were wooden flower boxes that seemed to be carved from different designs.

At Brelinbach we found a beautiful home of a Nazi party leader. He had acquired paintings, crystal, silverware, and so forth, from all over Europe. What made us mad was to find in his cellar American Red Cross CARE packages of food sent for American POWs. This guy took them home. As I stood there in all that wealth I thought to myself, "This guy may come home to find his home untouched and just start all over again when others across Europe are in ruins." I decided to even the score for the American POWs who never got their CARE parcels. I found a crowbar and smashed everything: mirrors, china closets, glass chandeliers, everything. People might think this was an awful thing to do, but at the time it seemed right to me. I was so mad, I even knocked the light switches out of the wall.

As we arrived in Shleusingen, the German troops had just left on a train. We entered a *gasthaus* and found beer mugs half full.

The Wehrmacht had left in a hurry. We reached an enclosure full of French slave laborers and took them to the *gasthaus* for some beer. The big fat German bartender sulked as we made him serve the French. When the keg ran out, he tried to say "*das ist alles*" (that is all). Larry Choiniere and I drew our .45s and yelled, "*Bringen mehr bier!*" (Bring more beer) and fatso got the message. He came back from the cellar with another keg and the Frenchmen shouted "*Vive la bière!*" Some of our squad started to call Larry and me SS 1 and SS 2 because of the action we could get by yelling at uncooperative Germans.

We were told that the objective of the Yankee Division was no longer Berlin. There was a strong rumor, put out by Dr. Goebbels no doubt, that Hitler would order his remaining forces to a Redoubt Area in the mountains of Austria. We were turned southeast to head them off.

Somewhere along these rolling hills, we came over a rise and several miles ahead of us were thousands of prisoners being herded eastward by German troops. When the Germans looked back and saw us and heard our tanks, they started to spray all the prisoners with machine gun fire. It was unbelievable. By the time we got there, the fields were covered with bodies all dressed in the blue and white vertical stripe uniforms of a concentration camp. Thousands of dead lay everywhere. It was a sickening sight. I thought of the hope that must have risen up in the hearts of the prisoners when they saw Americans coming to rescue them and then to be slaughtered. We were standing around in shock at all this death when three Ukrainians who survived came up the road bringing a German soldier who had been one of the guards. He was a *Volkssturm* (People's Army) soldier with a striped *Volkssturm* armband on his left sleeve. He had a large bloody wound on the side of his head where the Ukrainians had apparently hit him with a pair of wire cutters one man was carrying.

I could not understand Russian, but they came up to me and by gestures made me understand that they wanted to borrow my .45 pistol to kill the guard. I said no, he is a prisoner—"*Nein, er ist ein Gefangene.*" They kept shouting and pointing to all of their dead comrades. I tried to make them understand that Americans don't shoot prisoners. They turned from me in disgust and walked down the road. The old German just stood there shaking in fear. It is a day I will never forget.

At Eisfeld we were moving down the cobblestone street accompanied by a Sherman tank. On the second floor of a house a young girl was waving at us. We thought this was strange. Why would a German girl be waving at us?

Suddenly, a second girl appeared with her and they raised a *Panzerfaust* (German bazooka) to the windowsill to shoot at the tank. Maybe no one taught them how to fire the weapon, or else in their excitement they fumbled it.

Two guys from L Company were flushing out the house and came into the room behind them. The girls were still defiant after they were captured. They were not wearing *Volkssturm* armbands either.

We were rolling along on a scout patrol in advance of the main column near Koppalsdorf when out of a pretty white farmhouse emerges a German colonel in his dress uniform. He held up his hand to us as if motioning for a taxi and said goodbye to the people in the farmhouse. He got on the back of our truck and sat in the middle of the ammo pile. He was so clean and resplendent in his green uniform with white piping and elegant peaked cap. We soon learned that he could speak fluent English, and he complained about how dusty we were and admonished us not to brush against his clean uniform. Talk about arrogance! We were mad.

For some reason that day we had Sergeant Filsinger along with us. He was a supply sergeant back at battalion and had never been up front. He was seeing his first German soldier up close, and he was in awe. Filsinger started to ask the officer questions, and the colonel struck up a conversation with him since he deemed him to be a gentleman because his uniform was not dirty and dusty like those of our squad members. He showed Filsinger pictures he had taken in Poland and Russia where they hung Poles and Russians on every light pole in a town. He was very proud of the pictures. After I looked at them I asked the colonel why they hung those men. He said, "They are not men, only dogs. All Russians are animals."

I said to Pee Wee Moore, "Maybe we should teach this man some manners. Get a rope." Pee Wee caught on right away, but the German just laughed. Pee Wee came up with a small tent rope. I said, "That's too small, get a gun rope." So Pee Wee got out one of the heavy ropes used to pull the 57 mm gun. When we fastened a noose around the colonel's neck he began to whimper.

We stopped the truck and there up on a hill was a big tree with a stout branch extended just like you see in a Western movie. Our whole squad got out of the truck and moved up the hill pulling the German along. About the time it hit Filsinger what was going on he started to shout, "Don't do this men, you'll regret this all your lives!" Of course we never intended to hang the colonel, only to scare him, but now we had Filsinger to contend with, and we let him think we hanged Germans every day.

We got up to the tree and now the German was crying, "My family! My children! Who will run my business?" I could not believe that he was concerned about a business at a time like this. I kept throwing the end of the rope up to the branch and letting it fall down. After the third try I turned to the German and said, "If we don't hang you will you promise to shut up?" He readily agreed. We all got back on the truck and the cowed German sat there quietly as we rolled along. Our lead truck was going back to the battalion CP so they stopped to take our prisoner along with other POWs they had.

As the colonel left our truck, he came alongside to reach up and shake hands with Filsinger. "All good to you my friend. You saved my life," he said as Filsinger shook hands and smiled. The German then ran over and got on the other truck. As it pulled away we could see him excitedly telling the other Germans all about his narrow escape and pointing back to us. We all chuckled, but we never told Filsinger that it was a joke.

One beautiful sunny day we were strung out in a field near a village. We had our gun parked under a tree near a small stream where guys were digging in all around, but we got careless and didn't dig in. I was enjoying the sunshine when I saw about five or six fighter planes hedge hopping toward us. I yelled, "Here comes our Air Force!" Just then the fighters started firing, and I realized they weren't P-47s but Luftwaffe ME-109s, and there I was with no hole to dive into.

It is a very naked feeling to be caught out in an open field and be strafed by fighter planes. In desperation I climbed under the gun carriage while all of the tanks nearby opened up with their machine guns. To our amazement, they managed to shoot down three of the planes while the rest high tailed it out of there.

When we got into the village of Wolfersdorf I went into a flour mill that was operated by a series of belts, pulleys, and wheels but no electricity. I looked out the side door to see a small stream rolling by. I heard about water power but surely, I thought, this small stream can't run this big plant. Being curious I went out and closed the sluice gate. I then came inside and slid the one belt closest to the door over a wheel. All at once the place started to roar and hum while the whole building shook. I looked around to see how to stop it but could not find any lever. Since I did not want to stick my hand under that spinning belt I just opened the door and left. Someone else must have shut it off later. At least now I understood about water power.

Our mail caught up with us, and I got a letter from my brother Bill in the Philippines. He said he thought I would read his letter in Berlin. "My," I thought, "but they are optimistic in the Pacific."

He said they had landed on Cebu, and the Filipinos were very glad to see Americans again. He included a picture of himself in his army suntan uniform. On the back he wrote, "From one fighter to another." I still have that photo.

At Gundelsdorn we found a lot of German vehicles abandoned along the road, out of fuel. Their benzine supply was going fast. "It couldn't be too long now," we all said but then we remembered the undying spirit of these fanatics, so we hitched up our belts another notch.

Our supply lines were getting longer and thinner as we stretched eastward, and we had to conserve our gasoline and so forth. We did not use many K- or C-rations since we ate canned or jarred food we found in German houses. We also found plenty of *eier*. We got them by the bowlful as the Germans looked on. Our chowhound Choiniere set the record by eating 15 fried eggs at one sitting.

I often wonder how many homes we had been in. Some for just a few minutes, some overnight, others for up to a week. Most of the Germans were upset when we moved in. Did they think we would set up tents in the field?

Early one morning we were sitting on the side of a hill watching the sun come up over a small village. We had just liberated a number of Polish slave laborers who were seated on the hill with us eating the food we shared with them. Someone passed word that President Roosevelt had died, and we were saddened that he did not live to see the end of the war.

It was April, 1945, and I thought to myself, "I have been in Europe now for eight months. How much longer will this war go on?"

There was an educated Polish man sitting by me and he spoke good English. He mourned the loss of Roosevelt and kept calling him "a gentleman, such a gentleman." I learned that most of the people in Europe knew who Franklin Roosevelt was and had a great respect for him.

Later on we moved off the hill and down into the village where we could not find a single civilian. Apparently they were all in church as it was Easter Sunday. Each squad moved into a house where we found Easter dinner already in the oven.

You should have seen the looks on the faces of the Germans when they came home from Mass to find a gang of Americans seated around their dining room table eating their Easter dinner off their best china. Then after they ate, the GIs opened the windows and threw the dirty dishes out in the yard. I'll bet that is one Easter those folks never forgot.

My sister Inez's husband Walter was a lieutenant in the 100th Infantry Division in Europe. To my surprise one day, we were moving along in a convoy when I noticed the numbers marked on the front bumpers of the vehicles that were coming down the road from the opposite direction. It was the 100th Division, so I began to watch for Walter's regiment numbers and all of a sudden there he was seated next to the driver of a $1^1/_2$-ton truck.

I screamed, "Hey Walter! Walter!" but he did not see or hear me as he was waving to some Russian POWs on the other side of the road. As we continued to move I yelled to a GI in the truck behind him to tell him my name and outfit. Just imagine the odds of running into each other and then not really meeting! When I wrote home, I told my family that I had seen Walter.

At Sonneberg we released a large group of Russian women slave laborers. They smashed open a clothing warehouse they knew about since they made the clothing and donned clean new blue blouses. They all looked so cute as they blew kisses to us as we moved out of town.

American soldiers loved to loot the German homes. We called it "liberating." It was comical to see infantrymen slogging along with their rifles over their shoulders and carrying a brass lamp, marble table top, china bowls, paintings, even tapestry. About a mile outside whatever town we had just left, the weight would begin to tire the GIs and they would toss their prize into the nearest ditch with a shrug. So what! We will pick up something else in the next town. If the German civilians had only followed us about one mile they could have recovered most of their belongings. To us it was a funny part of war.

It was no big deal, but we all noticed that we never saw an American flag all during combat. Maybe they put up the Stars and Stripes back at division headquarters, but I never got back there to see. We all talked about how in the movies back home John Wayne and the Marines always seemed to carry a flag to hoist over every hilltop.

It was somewhere near Oberfobach that we got into steep mountains. We were told our objective was a town on the other side of a mountain and that the road wound around a series of valleys to get there. Our job was to climb the mountain on foot and surprise the enemy from behind.

All day we hiked across a valley and it got so warm that you could follow our trail by the number of sleeping bags that were tossed aside. At one point I was going to pick one up because it might get cold again that night, but I was hot so I didn't.

When we got to the mountain we had to go hand over hand. Each man had to reach down and pull the next man up the incline. It was slow and laborious, but we kept going on up. I was carrying my bazooka, and it seemed to weigh a ton.

Finally, after dark we came down the mountain into the town to find that our tankers had come around the mountain by road and were occupying the place. As we dragged ourselves along the road some tankers came out of a house and said, "Here comes the infantry! You guys must be worn out. How about a drink?" I gladly took the offered bottle of schnapps and drank to get warm.

When we got into a house it was so cold that I wished I had picked up that sleeping bag back on the trail. What I did to sleep warm was to take all of the German civilian suits and coats out of the chiffonnier and pile them on top of me. GIs always know how to improvise.

The next day I remember how Bailey, who was from Alabama, as he could see the Alps in the distance, kept saying, "I don't see any sheep! Back in Alabama they told us in school that they raised sheep in the Alps. I don't see any sheep!" We all grinned because the Alps were too far away to see anything.

It warmed up the next day, and we had some rain. We were going along a muddy road through a wooded area when we took some rifle fire from the woods on the right. I got Pee Wee and Larry to go with me to find the snipers. I borrowed Bob Goad's carbine since I was wearing only a .45 pistol.

We flushed two soldiers out of the woods, and they ran down the hill away from us. Chasing them, we came to a clearing with a farm-house. Two women came out of the house and looked terrified.

"*Deutsch Soldat in das Haus?*" I asked.

"*Nein, nichts Soldat,*" they answered.

"Cover me you guys, I'm going inside," I said.

I kicked open the door, which led into a kitchen. A little old Ger-man woman dressed all in black with a safety pin at her neck held up her right hand nervously and said, "*Heil Hitler!*"

I yelled, "*Deutsch Soldat in das Zimmer?*" pointing to a pantry door.

"*Nein*", she said.

I kicked open the pantry door and burst into the small room with my carbine ready to fire.

As I looked to my left, the two German soldiers were standing against the wall. I swung my carbine to cover them, and it stuck. I looked down quickly to see that the carbine sling, a heavy-duty canvas strap, had caught on the white porcelain knob. I could not cover the soldiers unless I got the strap loosened.

I still don't know where I got the idea, maybe from some old movie, but I faced the two Germans and screamed at the top of my lungs, "AAAOOGHH!!!" It stunned them into a freeze as I untangled the sling and covered them with my carbine. "*Raus!*" I shouted and pushed them past old grandma who was shrieking and crying.

Pee Wee was holding the two women at pistol point, and they began to cry as I appeared with the two soldiers. They thought we were going to shoot them all when Larry and Pee Wee lined them up while I looked around for more snipers.

We figured that these two soldiers must have been relatives and that they had retreated to their home. The women stopped their cry-ing as we led our two captives back through the woods. For the rest of my life, I have thought of that incident every time I see a white porce-lain knob anywhere.

All of the towns of any size had a number of rich homes that any-one could see were the homes of the most important Nazis. When you ever attempted to question these Hitler lovers they always came back with a stock answer, "Who me? No, not me." When you told them about the concentration camps and the atrocities they would say, "Oh, no, not German soldiers. They are gentlemen."

At Hildbrandgrund we learned that this was the area where all those stories about knights and dragons were supposed to have taken place.

At Munchberg we recaptured a lot of American jeeps that the Germans had taken from us during the Battle of the Bulge. They had made good use of them against us and now we had them back.

At Sparneck a cute little Ukrainian girl who was a slave worker on a farm told us many stories of how she was mistreated by the Germans. She had not seen her family for three years. Many German families were given slaves to do their manual work. It reminded us of the Romans and how they used captured nations as sources of slave labor.

Near Heinersreuth and Wahl we saw all the big open uninhabited land around and we laughed at how Hitler said the Germans needed more living room. So much for *Lebensraum.*

We were in a farmhouse, and Sam Harper had drunk so much red wine that he got in an argument with Larry Choiniere who, as usual, was eating a big plate of fried eggs. Sam got out his double-edged trench knife with brass knuckles, which he had picked up in an old World War I trench while were in the Argonne Forest. He kept yelling that he was going to stick it into Larry. Larry kept yelling, "You're drunk Sam," which only made Sam angrier. His eyes were all red and he was really worked up. I pulled out my .45 pistol and got between them. I convinced Larry to stop telling Sam he was drunk. Robbie came in and got Sam to calm down. Sam was a real backwoodsman, and when he drank too much and got his temper up he could be expected to do anything. It did not take much to get Larry and Sam going against each other.

At Weissenstadt the German troops in the town had fired on us after flying a white flag from every house. Several of our guys were killed. We burned the town. What was left we lived in after we kicked the civilians out into the barns. We were in no mood to be fooled with that night. I remember one man and woman who ran back and forth from a water pump to their home with a wash basin as they tried to put out the fire. We just laughed at them. One of the guys said, "Maybe we should shoot holes in the pan?" but we didn't.

At Buchhaus we learned that we had overextended our front so we had to go back to Munchberg where we found a cellar full of champagne and some French laborers who directed us to a brewery. It was the first beer we had found in a long time.

It was a beautiful, warm, spring day as we roared through

Kirchlamitz. On the road we saw a jeep with a red metal sign with two silver stars. Wow! A major general this far forward must mean that the war is winding down.

At Weiden we stayed in a big hotel along with some French, Czech, and Hungarian workers. We had plenty of beer and eggs. Late that night a German patrol came up near our 57 mm gun and several of our guys cut them down after a chase through a field. Later, Larry Choiniere came back with some donuts he found in a bakery and we made short work of them.

Then came the day that we rolled up to the edge of the Danube River. At last, we had run out of German land to conquer.

7

Czechoslovakia and the Surrender of the 11th Panzer Division

INSTEAD OF CROSSING THE DANUBE, WE TURNED northeast and headed into more German territory. It was somewhere near Kabreuth that we hit strong German resistance and several of our tanks were knocked out.

We were under some artillery and mortar fire when I got knocked down with a SLAM to my head. I picked myself up and had a ring in my ears but could see no blood. When I took off my helmet, I burned my hand a bit on a jagged piece of hot shrapnel that had slammed into my helmet. The prayers back home were still working as a piece of the shell burst through my steel helmet but was stopped from entering my head by the helmet liner. Praise the Lord!

A little later I pulled the jagged blue metal shrapnel out of my helmet and saw a hole about two inches long. I showed the helmet and shrapnel to Lieutenant Deviese and Sergeant Piquette with the laughing comment, "Here is another man's life saved by his helmet!" I was grinning, but they looked at each other very soberly as if to say, "Will Courtney ever take this war seriously?"

We moved into a house in the corner of the town square and started to fry up some eggs on the kitchen stove. There was an old German grandmother typically dressed all in black with a brooch pin at her throat. She was trying to tell us how to cook eggs and was really getting in the way. We had just received orders not to fraternize with the civilians and to make them live on the upper floors of their homes. I said, "*Kommen Sie Grossmutter,*" and led her to the steps to go up-stairs. She protested loud and vigorously that she would not go up-stairs. Believing that she was being arrogant and stubborn, I coaxed her up the stairs until she turned to come to a landing. Then I saw why she did not want to go upstairs.

Lying on her back, with her head on the landing and her feet up on the stairs, was a beautiful blond girl about 18 years old. Her eyes were open and staring while a trickle of blood drained from a bullet hole right between her green eyes. Her blond hair was braided with the ends tied in blue ribbons. She was wearing a peasant costume with a laced bodice and white blouse with puffy sleeves. She wore a short white apron over her blue skirt and had high-top laced shoes. She was so beautiful, even in death.

I stepped past her and went up to the second floor of the home. The second floor was one big room with a gorgeous hard-wood floor. The windows exuded charm from the small diamond-shaped panes that were fitted into oak wood frames. In one of the front window panes was one bullet hole about the right size for a .30 caliber round. I tried to reconstruct in my mind what had happened here. I reasoned that the girl's curiosity drew her to look out the front window as the tanks and infantrymen entered the square. When you are flushing out a town, your nerves are on edge and you have a tendency to shoot at anything that moves. Some GI likely caught sight of a person moving behind the diamond-shaped panes. Then, remembering the two girls who tried to shoot one of our tanks with a *Panzerfaust*, he fired a shot. As the girl was hit with the bullet, she must have, by instinct, tried to run back down the stairs but fell dead as she got to the top of the steps. How sad, I thought. If only she had not been curious enough to look out, she would be alive.

I went back down the stairs to my squad and explained everything. We did not make *Grossmutter* go upstairs again but let her stay in the kitchen.

We moved on to Putzeleim where we heard a wild rumor that the war was all over. No one believed it but secretly hoped that it was true. Some liberated Frenchmen were already celebrating. From our experi-ence we learned that it didn't take much to get them to do that.

At Altenfelden we left the Reich and entered Austria, another coun-try for us. Our military government people arrived and posted procla-mations all over the town. Since many Austrians served in the German army, either by choice or by force, many of the civilians were sympathetic to the German cause. We didn't see any difference between the Germans and the Austrians, perhaps because they all spoke German.

It was a dark somber-looking day, and Miller from L Company gave me the sweatband out of his helmet liner to use in my replacement helmet. This of course gave him an excuse once again to go without a helmet. I wonder how many helmets he managed to lose during the war.

We camped out near Neufelden, and to get warm we had a small fire of tiny logs from a nearby fence. I fell asleep next to the fire and burned my pants and boots.

At St. Johann Wimburg, we were near the Danube and stopped along a small tributary stream with steep walled banks. We hunkered down in the misty rain by a small fire and were amazed to see once again a jeep with a two-star general pass by. Now we began to believe that this war must be getting close to the end.

As we passed through Piberschlag, some Polish girls who had been freed from a labor camp came out to the column and gave us big bunches of fresh flowers. It was nice to see these girls who had been so mistreated smile with shining eyes as they passed us the bouquets.

We stopped for the night in the village of Hinterwiebenbuch where Duquette and I decided we wanted to eat chicken. We went out to find some and returned with four hens, which tasted mighty good after they were fried. Later we moved slowly near Gugwald northbound on tortuous mountain roads that resembled old wagon trails. Even today there is no road on the map but only a forest trail. We crossed the border at Heuraffel and entered Czechoslovakia.

We set up our antitank gun near a house at the edge of town, and some girls came out to talk to us. We tried to learn phrases of Czech, but it was too hard for us so we stuck to the German phrases we had learned. To our surprise, we thought that these people would all want to be known as Czechs, but we were mistaken. When questioned, they said, "*Nein, wir sind Deutsch*" (No, we are German).

Later we realized that we were in the Sudetenland, that portion of Czechoslovakia that went through a plebiscite in 1938 to vote whether or not to join with Germany. We found that most of these people wanted to be German.

As we crossed the Muldau River on bridges that the Germans had failed to destroy, I remarked how much it looked like the Juniata River back home near Altoona.

Later, in Morowitz we set up our guns alongside a cemetery wall on a hill with a commanding view of the whole valley. We marveled at the little monastery perched on the overhanging edge of a cliff. I remember how Miller and his squad dug in next to our foxholes and how he talked a little boy into getting a blanket for him to use in his hole. He said, "Tell your mother she will get the blanket back in the morning."

That evening he put on a show for all of us plus some civilians who lived nearby. "*Seit Hitler kommt, keine schokolade, nichts viel essen, kein benzin, viel arbeiten. Oh Hitler nicht gut für Deutschland. Amerikaners sind besser. Amerikaners haben gut soldats,*" and so forth. He did this in a pleading voice with gestures. We all laughed because we had heard this from many Germans as we crossed their territory.

In a dense woods near Bramles, we brought in a large number of German prisoners. Two of the SS troopers got into a fight over the surrender, as they had not wanted to give up, so our guys let them fight it out with their fists. It ended up with Bailey and Duke each slugging an SS man.

It was early in May now. The sun was warm and the sky was blue. We were moving up the narrow valley along the Muldau River. Red Hubert, Larry Choiniere, and I were out in front of our column about two miles and walked into a small village named Ebenau. We were supposed to be the point and look for German troops. We were told that we might run into the Russians as they were reported to be coming from the east.

We were standing in the middle of a dusty road enjoying the sunshine when we heard the rumbling noise of an approaching armored column. We froze. All we had between us were two carbines, one .45 pistol, my bazooka, and the hand grenades that hung from our jacket lapels. We had no radios or communications of any kind to call for help. As we looked up the road, here came the column led by a Tiger tank. Choiniere asked, "What shall we do now, Courtney?"

I said, "Well, we can fire the bazooka and it will bounce off the front of that Tiger tank like a Ping-Pong ball. Then they will open up with their machine guns and spray us down. Why don't we just stand here, look tough, and see what happens." So we did.

The tank was coming straight at us and we had mixed emotions as we stood there. When the tank was about a hundred yards from us, a green Mercedes Benz staff car darted around the tank, drove up, and stopped next to us. The back door opened, and a German colonel got out and held the door for the general who got out, saluted me, and offered to surrender the 11th Panzer Division to us!

We kept our cool and directed them to order the rest of the column to turn left down an embankment and line up in the big meadow. They complied readily. The Germans seemed to be relieved to surrender and became very docile and cooperative. We got them all to stack their rifles on a pile, line up their armor in rows, and then had all the troops line up in a formation with their hands on their heads as we frisked them.

We got so many wristwatches that Red Hubert took off his helmet to use as a container to hold them. We also liberated their knives, even penknives. I got a penknife engraved *Adolph Hogrebe* that I still carry in my pocket today. It is OK except for a chunk that came out of the blade where I tried to use it like a bayonet to cut open the wire strap on a 10 in 1 ration box.

One nattily uniformed officer tried to give me the German money in his pocket but I gave it back. We had no use for money though later we wished we had it. Altogether we had several hundred prisoners, and we were wondering what to do next when suddenly a jeep appeared on the road. The driver took one look, turned around quickly, and roared away to the rear.

About an hour later, a small American convoy arrived with two command cars full of senior officers. They drove onto the meadow and pulled up in front of the German formation. As the American officers got out of the cars, the German officers with the general and colonel came to the front and saluted. The American officers saluted and they all shook hands.

Meanwhile the three of us, all privates, were ignored. This was OK with us as we were eager to get out of there and split up our loot. While the formal surrender was taking place, Red, Larry, and I went into the one-room pub in Ebenau and piled all the watches and pistols (which we had put in a bag) on top of the big round table. We split everything three ways. Larry took a long time to see if he wanted a black-face watch or one with a sweep-second hand. I ended up with the black-faced *Heloise* wristwatch, and I wore it for years. I still have it in my dresser drawer.

All three of us wore wristwatches up to our elbows on both arms. We had all kinds as the Germans had taken them from Poles, French, Czechs, and so forth. Later I gave most of mine to former slave laborers as my way of evening up the score.

The rest of our platoon moved up and joined us at Ebenau where we stayed about a week. It was here that we got word on May 7th, 1945, that the war was over.

We stood around this tiny village of seven or eight houses and wanted to celebrate but had no booze. The tiny one-room pub was empty. We could imagine the big celebrations they must be having in Paris and New York, but not here. We felt cheated.

After dark that night, the rest of the 11th Panzer Division arrived to surrender. We were amazed to see how much armor they still had left, and it took hours for the column to pass through to our rear. One of the German soldiers on a truck that had stopped in the column yelled out in French, "Who speaks French?"

"I speak French!" I shouted.

"Are the Russians in Krummau?" he asked.

"No," I said, "in Budweis [Budjovce]," and the column moved on.

As it turned out, the reason that the Germans surrendered to us was that they wanted to surrender to Americans before the Russians caught up to them. The Russians came into Budweis about ten miles east of Krummau while we moved up and occupied Krummau, now known as Český Krumlov.

As the German columns moved through our lines, we were surprised to see how many women soldiers they had. All the fight was gone from the Krauts, and they looked relieved to be captured by Americans. They had all heard of the atrocities committed by the Russians on the eastern front and knew the Americans adhered to the Geneva Convention.

After the 11th Panzer prisoners had been escorted down the dusty road to the rear, our platoon was left in Ebenau. The war was over, and all at once discipline seemed to end. We had fought and won the war, but no one seemed to have a plan for peace.

We just wandered around the fields and fished in the Muldau River, this time with a pole and line instead of hand grenades.

Once more the big, tough GIs reverted to being little boys. Guys would climb up the side of the meadow, maybe two or three at a time, then lay down and giggle out loud as they rolled down the hill to the bottom. Then some would tickle each other and giggle and laugh as if to eliminate all the fear and tension.

Another thing happened. When the push forward stopped, when we were no longer attacking, the supply line stopped too. It was almost as if everyone stopped in place, and no one realized that we still needed food to be sent forward. It took about a week before it got started again. Meanwhile we used up all the field rations.

Several times I went out in a field and pulled up radishes, carrots, and onions to eat. We got some wheels of black bread from the civilians, but they must have gotten word about us here because they sure had their eggs hidden.

A few days later, Sergeant Beck came down the road from Krummau riding in a Russian jeep along with two Russians. They stopped while Beck and I talked. He said, "You ought to toss these guys a highball (salute)." I decided not to do so, and they continued to the rear. Later that day, a long column of German prisoners came back up from our rear and headed north toward Krummau. We were mystified until the next day when Lt. Walter Cody came by and told us that all those Germans who had surrendered to us were turned over to the Russians.

We all voiced our view that this was a dirty deal and that those Germans had trusted the Americans to accept their surrender. Lieutenant Cody agreed with us, but he did not know who had decided to transfer the POWs to the Russians.

We were told to guard the road and to allow no one to head south to our rear. The next morning I was on guard when three Yugoslavs came along pushing a boy's express wagon with all their belongings on it. They explained to me that they were going home and showed me their flag. I told them it was *verboten* but maybe they should try again tomorrow. They understood and went up on the hillside to camp for the night.

Again the next morning, I was on guard and they came again. I felt sorry for them and could not understand the order to close our line, so I told them it was still *Verboten* to go south. Then I held my hands over my eyes and said, "*Verboten*." They all thanked me at once and started pushing their wagon down the road. I often wonder if they made it all the way back home to the Balkans.

Larry Choiniere and I were walking up the road toward Krummau when we spotted a German truck that had been run off the road down the hill into some heavy brush. It turned out to be loaded with loaves of bread. We told the civilians in Ebenau about it and soon the women went up the road wearing back packs. Soon they came back all smiles and their packs loaded with bread.

One night I was on the road, and I ran into a squad of Russian soldiers. They seemed happy to find an American and got me to go to a house where they were staying. Although none of us could understand each other's language, they insisted that I eat one of their food items. It was a greasy meat chunk about two inches square, and it did not look very appetizing or even sanitary. They seemed to want to give me something, and I did not want to insult them by refusing, so I choked it down. It tasted awful, but I grinned real big and said,

"GOOOOD!"

At this they tried to get me to eat another one, but my stomach had enough and I politely resisted all of their entreaties. I gave them the few cigarettes I had, and we shook hands all around and then I got out of there. So much for allied relations.

We moved up the dirt road north of Ebenau and came to the village of Potsmühle where we broke open a slave-labor camp of mostly Polish women and a few old men. The women screamed for joy as we peeled back the barbed wire gate. We gave them whatever K-rations we had to eat, and they smiled their thanks.

Since there was no place to go, the Polish stayed there in the camp but did not have to go and work every day. The first night we were there, the women asked our squad to come into the mess hall, which was a long one-story building with some long wooden tables in it. The women had picked flowers and put them into bottles. Also they had some candles in bottles to light up the room. They began to sing in Polish, and one GI told everyone they were singing the Polish national anthem, *"Marsh, marsh dombroski, ja va los la Polsky!"*

When they finished the anthem, we all clapped and cheered. Then the women motioned to us to sing the American national anthem. We all looked at each other. "Does anyone know the words to the '*Star Spangled Banner*?' I asked. No one did. "OK. Let's sing '*God Bless America*.' They won't know the difference." So we did very enthusiastically. The women had tears of joy in their eyes, and soon all of us did too. It was a moment none of us will ever forget. Here were men and women who had been prisoners and slaves in a barbed wire cage for years, and now we had come and set them free. We remarked that it was too bad that all the men we had left behind in the mud and snow could not be here to see this. It was a feeling of exhilaration.

We lived in the camp for several days, and I tried to learn some Polish words. The Poles laughed as I tried to pronounce the phrases. I did learn to say "Thank You" and "Good Morning" from an old woman named Tekla Traheimiak.

I remember one older Polish man who was tall and slender and had a mustache and glasses. Wherever he went, he always carried this worn old briefcase. He had been a professor at Warsaw University, and he always tried to maintain his dignity. The briefcase was his badge of distinction, and the other Polish people always showed him deference and respect.

Most of these people were forced to work in the paper mill near Potsmühle, which we were told was one of the largest in Europe. Many of the women were sent out as houseworkers, street cleaners, or farm workers. At least they looked healthier than those gray, emaciated prisoners we had seen in other camps across Germany. I lost count of how many camps we opened up and then had to live in ourselves for days until we moved on.

In a few days our platoon moved to Krummau, which was a beautiful and historic town of several thousand people. A large castle dominated the city as it hung on a cliff over the Vlatva River. With its battlements and round towers with pointed spires it looked just like those pictured in our history books back home.

We were a very thin occupying force of about thirty men. However, the people of Krummau thought we were great and treated us with respect. Our squad was quartered in a dairy building on the north of town. We lived upstairs in a makeshift dormitory, and every morning an old man would carry up a can of fresh milk to our floor.

We maintained a guard post on the road in front of the dairy. The cobblestone roadway was lined with big trees on both sides. We carried out two overstuffed chairs and set them next to the road. We sat in these chairs with our feet up on the trees and our rifles leaning against the trees. The local civilians thought Americans were very unmilitary. After all, they were used to the military precision of the German army. We would laugh and tell them we were citizen soldiers and not professionals. They would shake their heads and say they could not understand how the Americans had won the war.

Just up the road about a mile from us was a large field full of German POWs guarded by two GIs with a .30 caliber machine gun. The German officers in this group were permitted to keep their pistols, supposedly so they could control their troops.

One morning we were greeted with a soft, warm rain, very light, sort of a drizzle. As Frank Chapo and I stood our tours as guards on the tree-lined road, we heard the sound of marching feet.

As we looked to the east and the sound of the marchers, we could see a long column of uniformed men approaching, four abreast. They were wearing field gray uniforms but did not look like Germans.

At the head of the column was a soldier carrying a large white flag on a pole. The expressions on the faces of the men were very sad and grim. Chapo could speak Hungarian and yelled out to the column. One of the men apparently could understand Hungarian and told Chapo that this was a column of the White Russian Army who had fought against the Russian Red Army.

Chapo explained to me that they knew that their days were numbered if the Americans turned them over to the Russians. I remembered reading about the White Russians who opposed the Communist Reds when the Soviet Union was formed and how the Reds had butchered so many of them then.

Chapo and I both agreed that we thought that our authorities would soon turn them over to the Russians, which would mean either death or Siberia. We felt sorry for them. We never heard what happened to them.

One beautiful sunny day, a woman came walking up the road while Larry and I were on guard duty. She looked and reminded me of my mother. As she approached us, she was smiling and seemed to be so happy. She handed each of us a large bouquet of lilacs she had just picked. Then she gave each of us a big hug and a kiss and said, "*Danke, Amerikan.*" She then headed down the road in the direction of the POW camp. We both remarked about how happy she was and grateful that the Americans were here and the war was over.

Next morning we learned that there had been some action down at the POW camp, so Larry and I walked down to see what had happened. There on the ground lay the woman who had brought us the lilacs. She had been shot dead.

We asked the two GI guards for details and learned that the woman had approached the German officers and told them the war was over and they had lost and how happy this made her. Whatever else she said made one of the German officers so mad that he drew his pistol and shot her. We both were very sad to see our friend who had been so happy the day before now lying dead in the meadow. We never learned what if anything was done to the German officer.

One day I said to Larry, "Let's go see through that big castle." He said OK, so we walked through town and up the hill to the gateway. Inside the main gate was an office and a receptionist. She told us this castle dated back to 1224 and belonged to the family of the Prince of Schwartzenberg. In our best German we told her we wanted to go through the castle. She called on her phone and a man came out from a rear office, and she told us he was the director.

When we told him that we wanted a tour, he acted very put out and said he did not have the time. "Where has this guy been?" Larry asked. "Doesn't he know the Americans have captured Krummau?"

I looked at the director and with my right hand loosened the flap on my holster and put my hand on my .45. "We are going through and you can take us!" His demeanor changed. He summoned an assistant and the two of them led us on a tour of every room in the castle.

It was really something to see and the oil paintings were beautiful.

Several weeks later, we were told that tours of the castle for American GIs were being arranged and did we want to go? Larry and I said, "No thanks, we've already had our tour."

We got orders to change our guard post to the road that led to the Russian zone at Budweis. As we were pulling the gun through the narrow streets of Krummau, I was leaning backward out of the back of the truck trying to give clearance to Alfred Duquette, the driver. I yelled "OK. Go Ahead."

All at once, I was swept off the truck by a metal bar extending from a utility pole and dropped on the road between the truck and the 57 mm AT gun. The gun wheel rolled over my neck and back. When my fellow soldiers screamed for the truck to stop, I was sprawled flat on my back. The gun had dragged me and rolled me over from my back to my stomach and again to my back and I could not breathe. I thought I was dead. The whole squad gathered around, arguing about whose fault it was. To my relief, a young woman bent down and loosened my collar button and my belt and I began to breathe.

A crowd of civilians had gathered around to see what had happened to the American soldier. All of a sudden, a German jeep arrived and a German officer offered to take me to a doctor. They loaded me into the back of the jeep, and I gave directions to the driver how to get to our battalion headquarters, which was in a big white house.

As we drove through the town square, there was our platoon sergeant, Pinky Piquette, who looked at me as if to say, "What are you doing with those Germans?"

I yelled, "I was run over by the gun and they are taking me to the doctor."

The German lieutenant could speak some English, and we had a conversation about the life of a soldier in combat. We both had the same conclusion about war and the life of a soldier in it. When we got to the battalion CP, Colonel Dellert, the battalion commander, was there and he got mad at the doctor who was talking for a long time on the phone. "Get off that phone and look at this kid's back!" he ordered. With difficulty I took off my shirt and the doctor felt all over my back. "No broken bones. You'll be stiff for awhile, that's all," he said and dismissed me. No one offered to drive me back to my squad, so I slowly walked across Krummau to my squad location. I looked like an old invalid as I struggled along, and I was stiff for about two weeks.

One day as I walked along the street, I heard a young blond girl say something in French. So I stopped, went over to her, and started a conversation in French. Her name was Dora Balleghova, and she and her family came there from the city of Bratislava in Slovakia to escape the advancing Russian army. We became good friends, and later Dora even wrote a letter to my sisters Inez and Angela in French since I told her they studied French in high school.

From Dora I learned how the people of Slovakia considered themselves a separate nation and did not want to be part of Czechoslovakia. In recent years, they finally got their wish and are now a separate nation.

In Krummau we had milk, eggs, and butter, but the brewery was in Budweis so the Russians controlled it. We would send a party of GIs over to negotiate for beer, but the Russians only wanted to trade for wristwatches, which they prized. The Russkies would pay the highest prices for Mickey Mouse watches, up to $900 each!

At times the Russians would act like children. When they first came to a house that had a flush toilet, they thought it was a foot bath and would stand in the bowl and flush the toilet and giggle out loud. We heard later that the reason that the Russians always had so much Occupation money, schillings, was that someone had given them the plates that the United States Occupation money was printed with, and they also got a 10 to 1 trade ratio for their rubles. In effect, the United States taxpayer subsidized 90 cents on each dollar plus the fact that the Russians could print all the paper money they wanted.

One Russian soldier explained that he paid so much for a watch because at home the paper money was useless, but with a wristwatch to trade, he could buy a cow for his farm.

The civilians in Krummau were very fearful of the Russians who would roar into town and take anything they wanted at the point of a gun. The citizens of Krummau wondered why the American soldiers did not stop the Russians. We GIs wondered too. We had too few men to really protect the town, and we wondered why our army did not move up in force to occupy the area. Our policy appeared to be one to avoid provoking the Russians or causing an incident.

One day Lieutenant Deviese came up to our squad position and told us that the Russians were coming into Krummau every night to steal cars. He said we should round up any civilian cars we could find and drive them out to the edge of town facing Budweis and park them there for the Russians to find. "That way," he said, "the Russians won't have to come into town to steal cars and they won't terrorize the civilians."

I thought to myself, "What have we come to? Now we are to help the Russians steal cars. What a wishy washy policy this is." Of course, we were soldiers, and we had to obey orders even though we did not agree with the policy.

As soldiers we were not kept informed of events. We got all our news from civilians, especially about what the Russians were doing in eastern Europe. The civilians came to us one day with the story that the United States would soon go to war with the Soviet Union. They said, "See, you even have your big guns pointing east towards the Russian zone," which we did.

We started to get the *Stars and Stripes* again, and one of the stories showed American GIs in Berlin standing in line to buy $1,000 money orders to send home. They made all this money by trading watches with the Russians in Berlin.

We speculated how we too could make money if only we could get a supply of Mickey Mouse watches. I thought about writing home to my parents to buy a dozen or so watches and mail them to me. On second thought I realized that my dad would never do it as he would consider the idea too risky.

Also, I thought, by the time the watches would arrive here from the States we would probably be moved and have no more contact with the Russkies. Then I would be stuck with a box full of kids' toy watches.

The older men seemed more inclined to think up ways to make money as they needed it for their families at home. At age nineteen I was just happy to be alive and to smell the lilacs. My mother wrote that they were waiting to get a letter from me dated after May 8th, the day the war ended. She wrote, "Dare we hope?"

I hastened to write home that I was OK but did not tell them about being run over by the AT gun or else Mother would start to worry all over again.

Our squad got moved to a nearby village, Gojau, where we guarded a large number of German POWs. It was a grimy assignment, and we lived in a poor old shed of a building. We missed the beauty of Krummau and were glad when we moved back to the dairy building as soon as the Germans were moved out of the camp.

One night I was walking back alone from Krummau to the dairy and had to pass through the city gate and over the bridge across the moat. It was a beautiful moonlit summer night, and I was strolling along about midnight when out of the darkness of the gate came a man's voice, "Hey, Ami!" I became very alert and suddenly realized I could be in a dangerous situation here.

As I passed through the gate, which is a long opening in the city wall with cobblestone pavement and curbs on the sides, I could not see if there was more than one man inside. Because of the summer warm weather and the end of combat, I had stripped down from carrying a trench knife, cartridge belt, and the two hand grenades I always wore hanging from my collar buttons. I did however have my .45 caliber pistol in a holster hanging from my belt.

I had my right hand over the pistol as the man appeared out of the shadows. He looked to be about thirty years old and was probably a former German soldier out of uniform. Were there more in the shadows of the gate? Who knows? There were no Americans for at least a mile.

"Ami" he said, "let's Indian wrestle, like cowboys, you know?" He laughed and slapped his backside like he was whipping a horse. In English he said, "You know? Movies. Cowboys, Indian wrestle!" as he held out his hand.

I thought to myself, "What sort of a nut do I have here? Is he for real?"

So I grabbed his hand and we began to Indian wrestle back and forth across the cobblestone roadway inside the gate. I would push and then pull like we did as kids after we had seen a Tom Mix or Ken Maynard movie. Suddenly I caught him off balance and gave him a strong push and he fell over backward and landed with his head against the curb. He was laughing out loud and shouting, "Ami! Cowboys! Ja!" as I headed out of the gate and across the bridge out of Krummau.

As I continued my walk in the moonlight back to our dairy home, I laughed to myself to have found a fan of American cowboy movies clear over here in Czechoslovakia. Some adventure in the ancient walled city of Krummau in the summer of 1945.

Later our whole platoon was pulled back from Krummau to Wettern, a small village up on the hill overlooking Potsmühle, where our 3rd battalion CP was in a hotel next to a theater on the main road. Our whole company was quartered in a schoolhouse, and we had our company kitchen set up for meals. Soon we were griping that we ate better when we had to fend for ourselves in Krummau. We did not get as many eggs, as much milk, or as much butter. We also had to get back to company routine and military discipline.

Sergeant Beck got me the assignment of special services officer, although I was not an officer. I was supposed to come up with morale-building entertainment for our battalion. Lt. Ernest Tripp and I took a ride to 26th Division HQ to attend a session on how to put on comedy shows and use makeshift costume material. I ran into Fitzpatrick, the sign painter, from Fort Jackson days. He was the SSO for another battalion.

I went one day with Larry to the paper mill where we obtained large rolls of colored paper, which we cut into streamers to decorate the hall. We organized a small band to play GI music. We were all ready for a party as I got Sgt. Joe Sorrentino to hustle some buns, cold meat, and cheese. All we needed now were some girls, but there were only a few in the Wettern-Potsmühle area so I got three 1¹/₂-ton trucks assigned to me and we took off for Krummau. When we got to the town square I stood up on the hood of one of the trucks and shouted, "*Frauleins! Tanzen, musik, essen, heute abend in Potsmühle! Amerikanisch soldaten! Kommen Sie mit uns! Wir bringen Sie heim um elf uhr! Kommen Sie!*" (Ladies! dancing, music, and food tonight in Potsmühle! American soldiers! Come with us! We will bring you home at eleven o'clock! Come with us!)

You should have seen the girls pour out of the houses and climb into the trucks. I also saw many girls with their mothers trying to hold them back. I think the word that really sold them was *essen* (food) as the civilians had little to eat. We roared down the road and swung into the lot in front of the hotel theater complex to the welcome shouts of the assembled GIs. The whole crowd moved into the theater and the party was on.

One of my jobs was to hand out the sandwiches to the crowd and make sure that no one got two. This was quite a task and did not endear me to anyone. In my haste I gave one girl two sandwiches and Lieutenant Magee yelled, "Courtney, why did you give her two?" Before I could answer she melted into the crowd and was gone.

At the end of the evening it was hard to get all of the girls back on the trucks. Also some GIs insisted that they would go along. It was an old-fashioned singalong as we drove through the night back to Krummau. At the square we found most of the parents waiting and they hustled their daughters home.

I remember one night when we put on a dance just for the civilians of Potsmühle and Wettern. It had been against the law for anyone to dance by order of Adolf Hitler. When the music of our little band started up and the couples got on the floor I remember the gleam in their eyes as they took that first step. Almost as if they had forgotten how to dance but were ready to start again. I thought to myself, this too we freed the people from, a law against dancing.

At one of the concentration camps we opened as we came through Germany, Duke had picked up an SS police guard dog. The concentration camp survivors told stories about how these dogs were used against them and how vicious they could be.

Duke fed the dog and took him along in the truck. He soon became the squad mascot and jealously guarded our truck and gun from any intruders. When we moved to the schoolhouse at Wettern, Smokey, as we named the dog, stayed with us and became quite gentle. He used to romp and play with the neighborhood children. I remember looking out of the second floor window and seeing the boys and girls riding on his back and pulling his tail. He seemed to enjoy their attention and would run all over the schoolyard with the children. I thought to myself that this gives us hope. If that vicious guard dog, who had been trained to kill, could be changed by love and affection to a gentle playful dog, it is possible that those Nazis who lived on hatred and cruelty can be converted back to gentle, normal people. It would take time and patience but it could be done.

At Ebenau, the meadow where the three of us had the 11th Panzer Division park their tanks and trucks was changed into a recreation area. A huge oval track was constructed and competitive races were run. You should have seen the GI track teams compete in combat boots. The races between company teams became hot competition. One that I especially remember was a race where a major had obtained a pair of track shoes for his star athlete who then outdid the men running in combat boots. Lieutenant Murray became very red faced with anger as he protested this inequality with the major. Pulling rank, the major ruled that shoes were shoes. A sullen and angry Lieutenant Murray screamed, "Yes, Sir! Just as you say, Sir!" and walked back to his team. Lieutenant Murray had been reminded that he was still in the Army.

About this time the Army announced plans to begin to rotate troops home and that a point system had been designed. It gave credit for length of service as one of the criteria for discharge from the Army. This would have been acceptable to most GIs, but then the Army went further and gave five points for each medal or decoration. Wow! Did that set off the gripe sessions!

Now everyone looked back on opportunities to take Purple Hearts for being wounded or sometimes get a Bronze Star for some action. I thought back to Buderscheid in Luxembourg where I had refused a Purple Heart, which would have added five points to my score. The magic total one needed to go home first was 85 points based on time in service, time spent overseas, medals, and decorations. My total was only 60.

One sunny day we gathered around to say goodbye to all of our buddies who had 85 points as they boarded trucks to begin their journey home. Sergeant Pinky Piquette waved goodbye from his truck as they pulled away. My how we envied them. It was many years later that I learned from Pinky that they were shipped to England and worked there until December 1945. As it turned out, Pinky got home only three weeks ahead of me. That's the Army for you.

I remember the week that all the local civilians were upset because of a rumor that the American troops were all going to leave Czechoslovakia and that the Russian troops would replace us. Usually we found that the rumors the civilians heard were true. They usually got the facts before we in the Army did. My friend Dora told me that the local Bürgermeister had told all the people that they must visibly show the Americans how much they want us to stay. He told them to make American flags and hang them on their homes the next morning.

So the next morning we were greeted with the Stars and Stripes everywhere. How hard they must have worked that night before to find and cut material and in some cases dye it red, white, and blue. Since they never saw an American flag, as we never had any, they went to history books to find what it looked like.

Some of them used really old history books as some of the flags had only 24 stars and some had 13 stars in a circle. There were all kinds of combinations, but the message was clear. They liked the Americans and wanted us to stay. The other message was clear as well. They feared having the Russians occupy their country. We all expressed our thanks to as many civilians as we saw. There were smiles all around; however, the civilian grapevine was correct again. We received orders to pack up all our gear and say goodbye as we were going to be moved to Austria.

In the next few days there was much going here and there as we all said farewell to the many civilians we had gotten to know as friends. There were many tears as girls said goodbye to their GI boyfriends. Promises were made to write often. This was not farewell to a conquering army but goodbye to fair and friendly soldiers who impressed the Czechs and Slovaks with their positive American qualities.

It was a sad column of American GIs who rode south out of beautiful Czechoslovakia.

8

On Our Way to Another War

IT WAS ABOUT THE MIDDLE OF JULY WHEN I had been selected as a part of an advance team to go to northern Austria to arrange for billets for our troops. Our new, young company commander had sort of taken a shine to me as he enjoyed my jokes. He told me to drive his jeep and so I did, not bothering to tell him I had never gotten a GI driver's license. I had driven a car at home so I figured I could drive a jeep.

Early one sunny July day we headed south and east toward Austria. We sweated a lot because we had not been issued summer uniforms and still wore our ODs (olive drab, woolen). Somehow we did get away from General Patton's insistence on wearing ties, but while we wore our top shirt button open we were not allowed to roll up our sleeves.

We retraced our steps through parts of Germany along the winding curves and hills until we reached the Danube River. We crossed the river on a temporary wooden truss bridge that our engineers had fashioned to replace the stone arch structure that the Germans had blown up during their retreat. We had a small column of three jeeps and a 1¹/₂-ton truck pulling a 57 mm AT gun.

We entered the ancient city of Passau and twisted and turned through the city on old cobblestone streets. It was a beautiful city and had not been damaged by the war as the Germans had been retreating too fast to put up any defense there.

There is a long hill leading up from the lower part of the town to a plain above the city. I was following the truck and AT gun which Jackson, from our platoon, was driving. Several times on the hill he slowed up to shift to a lower gear and I, with great difficulty, was able to slow in time and change gears without hitting him. Later Jackson told me how much he enjoyed the ride up the hill and his causing me to shift gears so much.

He knew I had not driven a jeep before, and he said he told the other men on the truck, "Old Courtney must be going nuts by now with all this downshifting." They all enjoyed my discomfort.

Later, we were up on the plain and crossed the border into Austria. There was a pretty straight stretch of road, and we were rolling along, and I was in the midst of telling the captain a story when suddenly Jackson slammed on his brakes! I immediately slammed on my brakes but, since I was following too closely, I did not have enough room to stop in time and I plowed right into the barrel of the 57 mm gun.

The captain's eyes lit up and he laughed as we all got out to survey the damage. The gun seemed to be OK but the grill of the jeep was pushed in and had a nice round ring where the gun barrel hit it. Fortunately, the gun barrel had not pushed through into the radiator, so we were able to continue. I made some flip remark about the jeep's needing the brakes fixed but did make sure that I kept plenty of distance between Jackson's truck and my jeep for the rest of the trip.

We climbed southeastward into the hills of Upper Austria until we arrived in the village of Schardenberg. It sure wasn't much of a place and was far removed from anywhere.

To my amazement we were going to replace some Army Air Force troops who were billeted in some long, one-story buildings that were probably built to house slave laborers for the area. I reported in to the Air Force lieutenant and he showed me around the buildings where our company would be living when they arrived.

When we got back to his office, which was at the end of one of the barracks, the enlisted men told him that they had caught a local civilian stealing coal from their coal box and wanted the lieutenant to decide how to punish him. There was another man there, a civilian who spoke fluent English, and the lieutenant said to tell him not to do it again. The man related this in German to the culprit and the two of them started to walk away when I spoke up. Somehow I got the idea that I had to impress these Air Force guys that we were the 26th Infantry and a tough bunch of guys. "Hold it!" I shouted and motioned for the two men to return. When they came back to the barracks where the lieutenant and his Air Force enlisted men were I said to the civilian who spoke English, "Tell him we are infantry troops who are moving in here and if he ever steals coal from us we will shoot him! Make him understand that!" I said forcefully.

The man related this to the, by now, thoroughly cowed man, and I could see by their faces that the lieutenant and the fly boys were very impressed. I felt pretty cocky that I had scored one for the infantry.

A day later our battalion arrived in convoy and we all settled in for what we thought was going to be boring occupation duty. We got busy cleaning all of our weapons. Cleaning my pistol or carbine was not too bad, but I sure hated to clean the 57 mm AT gun. We had to jam rags and cleaning powder in the barrel and then use a ramrod to jam all this through the barrel of the gun over and over. Finally we would wad up a rag saturated with oil and ram it down the barrel to finish the cleaning.

The breechblock was the worst part because it was so heavy. Since I was number two man on the gun crew, I had to hold my knee up under the breechblock as the pins, that held it in place were pulled out. Then I had to lower and catch the block as it dropped out of the gun.

We then set it down and scrubbed and sanded it with crocus cloth and ended up greasing the whole block. To reinsert the breechblock in the gun meant that I put it on my knee as I crouched under the breech and pushed it up into the gun until the locking pins were replaced.

As a result, my pants were always greasy black. You could always tell who was number two on an AT gun crew. I remember Sgt. Jim Moorehead of the A & P platoon used to laugh and ask "When are you going to change your oil, Courtney?"

The scenery around Schardenberg was rural and made up of rolling hills. One day when we woke up, we were amazed to see the Alps as if they had just been moved right next to us. One day you could not see them and then, there they were, just as if a large painting had been dropped on the horizon. We could clearly see the snow on the peaks and the steep rocky sides.

When we asked the local civilians about this phenomenon they told us that this meant we would soon have rain. *"Sehen die Alpen bringen das regen."* The next day it poured rain all day, and the next day, and the next. Soon all the roads and pathways were muddy. It was miserable and we all said, "Take back your view of the Alps. Let's have our sunshine again."

Whenever we moved our base location it always seemed to foul up the mail delivery. It used to take weeks for a letter to arrive from the

States. V-Mail was somewhat faster.

Someone had come up with the idea of photographing letters and flying the film across the Atlantic. They named it V-Mail. Everything was V for victory in those days.

How it worked was that civilians bought a V-Mail form, which was one page about the size of a note pad which folded in half. They wrote their letter on the inside half, then folded and sealed the form and addressed it to the GI, added a stamp and mailed it. All servicemen's mail out of the U.S. went to Army or Navy post office numbers. Mail to our 26th Division was addressed to APO 26 (Army Post Office, 26th Division).

Wherever APO 26 was located, such as New York, they would open each V-Mail letter and photograph the page. Then all the letters on rolls of film would be flown across the Atlantic to the 26th Division headquarters. There the film would be printed on new V-Mail forms, folded in half, resealed and distributed to the proper company. Each company had a mail clerk. Our man was Vic Beaumonte from Williamsport, Pennsylvania. He would sort our company's mail and deliver it to each platoon where the squad leaders brought the letters to each man in his squad.

While the V-Mail letters came faster, no one ever really liked them because they were so small and only about a half page in size. People writing on a V-Mail form would try to write small so that they could get more in the letter and as a result the ink, when photographed, would be blurred and hard to read. Also, many wives and girl friends, knowing that their letters would be opened and photographed, were inhibited in what they wrote and the message usually was very bland. GIs always preferred a real letter from home even if it took longer.

I was reminded of the time back at Fort Jackson, South Carolina, when our company was assigned for a week to guard prisoners from the stockade who went out on work details each day. Each one of us was assigned a prisoner to guard all day with our loaded carbine leveled at him. We were told by the stockade sergeant every morning that if our prisoner escaped that we would have to go into the stockade to serve the rest of his term. Most of us doubted that this could be true but we weren't going to take any chances.

For several days our prisoners were assigned to dump the trash barrels that came from all over the camp into a large landfill. We guards would sit on empty boxes, cradling our rifles, as we watched them. These were long and boring days under the hot Carolina sun.

Often the prisoners would hand the guards handfuls of comic books straight from the trash pile to read, or a pack of letters that GIs had thrown away. Wow! Those were some letters to read. None of those wives or sweethearts ever imagined that their letters would be reread by strangers, nor did the soldiers who neglected to tear them up before they threw them away.

The guys who had served on prisoner guard duty all made sure in the future that they tore up their mail before it was discarded. I wonder if anyone might have saved those V-Mail film negatives? What a history of wartime morale that could tell us today.

I remember also that when we were guarding the GI prisoners at Fort Jackson, we all remarked how we were given one prisoner per man and were encouraged by that sadistic stockade sergeant to shoot to kill if our prisoner tried to escape. In our morning briefing every day of that week when our company took its turn as stockade guards, he would tell us that if he came out and found us with some dead GI prisoners that we had shot he would give us "all the beer we could drink."

The stockade prisoners were not murderers. Mostly they were guys who had gone AWOL, or been late coming back from a pass, or gotten drunk in town and been arrested by the MPs. Yet we would see a truck of German POWs with one American guard. They would have the easy jobs of cutting grass or being life guards at the Officer's Club swimming pool. Usually the big, handsome, blond Germans of the Afrika Corps were picked for pool duty to the delight of the officers' wives.

One day we all laughed as we saw a group of German POWs getting up on a $2^1/_2$-ton truck. Then the American guard handed up his carbine to one of the Germans to hold while he climbed up on the tailgate of the truck. We all wondered why our Army was so soft on the German POWs and so hard on its own GI prisoners. Some questions are never answered.

One night I went with a driver to pick up a lieutenant who was attending a party at regimental headquarters. When we got there, the party room was empty except for the lieutenant and lots of half filled bottles. He offered us a drink before we left, so I filled a glass full of schnapps and poured it down. "Pretty good stuff," I said as I set the glass down on the table.

The lieutenant who had observed me pouring the glass of schnapps down the hatch without stopping asked, "Was that wine?"

"No," I said, "it was schnapps," as I refilled my glass and downed it again.

He looked at me with admiration and amazement as I walked out to our jeep. On the way back to Schardenberg, the cool night air had its effect on me and the schnapps and I began to sing. I sang all the way home and happily said goodnight as I stumbled out of the jeep. The lieutenant grinned as they drove away, and I had difficulty managing to get up the one step into the barracks.

The next day saw feverish activity as we were alerted to move out. Our occupation duty in Austria was short-lived as we were heading back to Germany. One day later, we all loaded on our trucks and headed north and west out of Austria.

I remember the long hill at Passau as we drove down to the lower town. Somewhat west of the city we stopped for a relief break alongside the Danube where there was a dam. I unstrapped my camera and took a picture of the broad expanse of water rippling in the sunshine. One of the packages from home that caught up to me contained my little Baby Brownie Special camera and several rolls of 127 film.

I can't remember the exact date, but it was somewhere about this time that censorship of our mail was announced to be at an end. Prior to this, when we wrote any letter, we had to leave the envelope open so that one of our officers could censor anything out of our letters before they were sent on. We never got them back to see what was censored, so we had no idea what was blotted out. Some officers blotted words out with a pen and others cut words out of the paper with a razor blade, even if this meant cutting words on the other side of the page.

Many years after the war, my former squad leader, Sgt. Vic Martin, came to my home for a visit and brought with him a letter I had written to him at an Army hospital after he was wounded at 88 Junction Crossroads near Buderscheid, Luxembourg. It had so many words cut out that he could not get the sense of the letter. With some difficulty, I filled in the words for him, and he let me keep the shredded letter, which I still have.

Our caravan moved westward through eastern Germany, and at one time, we rode on the Autobahn, Hitler's superhighway, which reminded me of the Pennsylvania Turnpike. Along the way, as we passed other American troops who were garrisoning German towns they all expressed their envy, thinking we were headed back to the States.

We drove through Munich, and I could not believe the destruction. It seemed that the whole city was rubble. By now, a lot of the rubble was raked into neat piles along the streets so that traffic could flow. I still remember the Munich City Hall with only the metal framework standing bare on top against the sky.

Somehow a group of German civilians got into the line of our convoy with an old car that seemed to be having engine trouble. It was right ahead of our truck in line, and when they slowed down again, Duke, our driver, who had become very impatient with them, rammed the back of their car. In a panic they managed to steer to the side of the road as we roared by and Duquette yelled, "Serves you right, you Krauts!"

All along our route back across Germany, we could see work parties still clearing rubble from destroyed buildings, roads, and bridges. Some of the cities were so devastated that I wondered how they could ever be rebuilt. Where do you start to find the sewers, water pipes, and power lines all mixed in with unexploded bombs, mines, and booby traps? I often wonder how many people were killed or wounded as the cleanup progressed. War was still taking its toll.

All across Europe, in all countries, the children loved the American GIs, and the GIs loved the kids. Whenever our convoy would stop, kids would appear from all over and grin and turn their eyes up pleadingly, "Hey Joe! Gumie? Schokolade? Cigarette for Papa? Gut American!" And the American soldier always gave them whatever he had, gladly, willingly. The folks back home would have been so proud if they had seen their sons and how well they responded to the children of Europe.

As our caravan climbed up into the hills and forests of Germany, we finally came to our destination, Dalherda. It surely must have been selected to make sure that the YD would be far away from everything. Dalherda was a desolate place being practically a village.

After living in buildings since the end of the war, we were dismayed to find ourselves living in tents, ones larger than pup tents and with folding cots so that we did not sleep on the ground, but tents nonetheless.

There would be no more passes to anywhere at Dalherda, and we soon found out why. We also learned why we were moved to this remote area. The 26th Division had been selected to go to the Pacific Area to start to fight another war against the Japanese.

This came as a shock to all of us. We thought we had fought our war and were lucky enough to have survived. Now we found that we were expendable. They were going to send the YD to the CBI (China-Burma-India) theater. We did not get an official announcement, but the grapevine ferreted out our projected route of travel—through the Mediterranean to the Suez Canal, the Red Sea, and the Indian Ocean, then on to the Pacific fighting area. This definitely was not the boat ride that we had all been looking forward to.

Our training began the next day in earnest. Discipline, which had been lax since May, suddenly tightened up and everything became very serious. We had daily hikes, bayonet drills, map reading, and weapons instruction. Of course, the mail from home stopped because we had moved. Our morale was not very high.

It was hot and dusty during the day but cold and damp during the night, and we had no heaters in the tents. It did not help matters much when we got our copies of the *Stars and Stripes* with stories and pictures showing other GIs floating down the Rhine on scenic tour boats, partying in Paris, or attending USO shows with real movie stars. We felt like the poor little castoffs of the American Army.

Also, after 210 days in combat, it becomes somewhat degrading to start basic infantry training all over again. I'll bet the letters we wrote home from Dalherda were not too happy. Our families were counting the days until we would come home, and now they learned that our Army days would be extended.

One bright spot occurred when we attended a GI show, not a USO show with professional entertainers, but a homemade show with our own guys as actors. Back in Czechoslovakia, when I was the Special Service man for our battalion, I went one day with Lieutenant Tripp to division headquarters at Prachatice where they put on a training session to show us how to make a comedy show out of homemade props. Fitzpatrick, from regimental headquarters, had taken copious notes. Using these notes for vaudeville acts, he recruited some bored GIs and in a few days of practice put together a show.

We assembled one night in the largest building in Dalherda and Fitz and his boys gave their best. It was hilarious! Guys screamed, laughing and applauding over and over. The home made costumes made it even funnier.

I remember the hit of the show was the poor timid GI who had to go to military headquarters to get something approved. There was a long table with three officers seated at it, a captain, a major, and a colonel. Their rank insignia were made out of colored paper and were so large that they covered their shoulders. This started everyone laughing as soon as the curtains were opened.

The timid GI came in from the left with a paper form in his hand, which he meekly laid on the end of the table. Each of the officers had a large wooden handle to represent a rubber stamp, and there were three ink pads on the table. The captain picked up the paper and stamped it with a loud bang and shouted, "Approved!" Next, the major took his stamp and pounded it on the form and shouted, "Approved!" Then the colonel took the paper and pounded his stamp on it and shouted, "Denied!" and threw the form in a waste can at the end of the table as the timid private walked limply off to the right. None of the three officers ever looked up from the table. Their timing was perfect! It was loud, simple, and funny. The audience roared its approval.

One great thing about the Army was GI humor. It was always there. In the worst situation or biggest foul-up (and there were many), there was always some guy who would come up with a remark that hit the nail on the head and made everyone laugh. GI humor was not always printable, but no matter how raucous, it always fit. The favorite subject of ridicule was officers. It was the great leveler for private soldiers, who often were put upon by officers, to make funny remarks about them behind their backs or out of earshot. I am sure that officers had things to say about some of the enlisted men too.

After about two weeks, there was a rumble that we were moving out. Rumors were wild that we were heading to Marseilles and the ship for the Pacific. This time, thank heavens, the rumors were wrong. First Sergeant McKittrick, who had been promoted from antitank squad leader, gave our company the word. The orders for the YD to go to the Pacific were changed. We were now ordered back to occupation duty in Austria.

The news was greeted with mixed emotions by all the men. We were all elated that we would not have to go into combat again. However, many men were saddened that we were going east to Austria again instead of going west toward France and a ship home.

I don't think anyone even looked back as our convoy drove out of the Dalherda camp. It was a warm summer day and we enjoyed the scenery as we came back to Passau again.

We even stopped for a break at the same dam on the Danube River, and I stood at the same spot on the riverbank and took a picture facing the other direction. It made me feel like a tourist.

This time our company did not go to Schardenberg but went on to the sizable town of Scharding. It was a quaint town with an ancient stone wall surrounding the entire city. You had to drive through many arched-gate buildings to enter the town proper, and I always marveled that our $2^1/_2$-ton trucks, by going slowly, could just squeeze through.

The only damage to Scharding was to the arched stone bridge over the Inn River to Germany, which had been blown up by the retreating

Germans. Our engineers had built a very fine wooden bridge made out of heavy timbers complete with a walkway and retaining wall.

Our convoy pulled into the town square and many Austrians came out to greet us. Austria, we are back!

9

Occupation of Austria and Operation Keelhaul

OUR HEADQUARTERS COMPANY WAS BASED IN Scharding, which was the largest town in the area. Third Battalion headquarters was in the Gold Cross Hotel located in the southwest corner of the town square. Part of our company was billeted in a big yellow stucco schoolhouse in the southern part of town. A high wrought-iron fence encircled the school.

Two platoons lived in another school building nearer to the center of town. I lived here on the third floor in a big room with single cots along the walls and a big window on the front facing the street. There was a sort of mini town square area in front of the school, which probably was used by the students for calisthenics and recreation.

We did not have any formations, such as reveille or retreat. We never had a parade. We did not need a pass to go anywhere, nor did we have any set time to be in the barracks at night. Discipline was rather loose.

Our occupation mission was to help get the civilian population back to normal and get things running again. Since there was no war damage in this area, all of the utilities were functioning.

The Austrian people were very friendly and glad to have the Americans as occupiers. They had heard stories about the oppression of the Russians to the east. We never felt any danger of attack and consequently no longer carried our weapons, or even sidearms, unless we were on guard duty at the barracks, headquarters, or the bridge over the Inn River, which was the border with Germany.

Most of our people were assigned to direct the efforts of the civilian government in governing the area. I was amazed at how much authority was given to the noncoms (non-commissioned officers). My squad leader Robbie Robinson had the mayor's office where he told the *bürgermeister* what to do on a daily basis.

I was visiting him in his office one day when he was directing the *bürgermeister* to arrange to have fifty trucks and drivers for the next morning to deliver foodstuffs. After the *bürgermeister* left the office I asked Robbie where the man was supposed to find fifty trucks. Robbie shrugged and grinned, "I don't know, but whatever I tell him, he always does." I thought, "What a simple way to occupy a country."

The biggest problem in our area was the large number of DPs (displaced persons) and Hungarian POWs and their families. They seemed to be living everywhere, in houses, barns, or in the fields. Since the weather was warm, shelter was not a big issue but would be if they were still there in winter.

Since I still had the duty of acting Special Services Officer, although still a Pfc., I was free to roam around the area and to charter a jeep and driver when I needed one. Some of the drivers used to give me a hard time about this. "Hey Courtney, when did you get to be important enough to have a jeep chartered for you?"

I got to meet and know a lot of Hungarians, and I found them to be a warm and friendly people. Most of their officers had their wives and children with them, which I thought was an unusual thing for an army. From them I learned about their experiences fighting the Russians on the eastern front. I could not speak Hungarian, but in some German and many hand motions, they showed me how the Russian soldiers never bothered to seek shelter behind a rock or tree, but came straight at them standing straight up. They said the Russians didn't seem to care about casualties.

They told me how the Russians would wedge their bodies in the treads of German tanks to stop the them. I found it hard to believe until later on I read stories of this.

While the Hungarians had no love for the Germans, they were fighting to keep the Russians out of their homeland. They told terrible tales of the rape of Hungarian women as the Soviets advanced across their country.

I could see how much the Hungarians loved their country and, in 1956, during the Hungarian Revolution, I wondered how many of these soldiers I met were involved.

On the Danube River at Passau, I got acquainted with officers of the Hungarian Navy whose ships were tied up to the piers. I never knew they had a navy, but they did. They treated me like a guest of honor, and I was invited aboard the flagship where I met the admiral.

This must have been some navy I thought as I surveyed the scene. The admiral was a man small in stature but elegant in his manners as he greeted me resplendent in his white uniform with brass buttons and gold epaulets. He even wore white shoes, and to top it off he had a long gold cigarette holder that he used as a baton.

We were in the grand salon of the ship, which had a Persian carpet and gold chandeliers. On a carpeted platform in the center of the room stood a grand piano draped with gold cloth and tassels.

It was a magnificent setting with the sunshine streaming in the portholes to light up the area. After the admiral warmly shook my hand, he offered me a seat on an elegant white covered chair with gold trim. The other officers in attendance brought in tall goblets of Rhine wine, and we drank a toast to America.

Then the admiral mounted the platform, seated himself at the grand piano, and after placing his gold cigarette holder and cigarette on a white ashtray, he began to play beautiful classical music. I was enthralled. It was a regular concert and the first classical music I had heard since I left the States.

After about an hour, we adjourned to the deck where I took my leave as graciously as I could and thanked him for the performance. The admiral could speak English and he asked me, ever so politely, if I could possibly obtain some newer American piano sheet music for him. I assured him that I would write home and ask my parents to send some to me. His face lit up in a wonderful smile as he thanked me.

That very night when I got back to Scharding, I wrote home to my mother and asked her to send some new sheet music for my friend. I think I should have given her more details about the need for the sheet music.

Several weeks later I received a large envelope from home and inside was one piano sheet music song. It was called, "Please Don't Say No, Say Maybe." I had never heard of it and neither had any of the other GIs I showed it to.

When I next went to Passau, I went down to the wharf and sought out the admiral. He was glad to see me, and when I gave him the sheet music, he went right to the piano, sat down, and played.

As he played a sweet tune, a love song, I sat there wishing I had received a dozen or more songs. It was a delightful interlude in my military career. It was a view of what peacetime life could be like and, as I drove over the rolling hills back to Scharding, made me think about what my life would be like after I returned home to Altoona. As it turned out, that was the last time I would ever see the admiral and the remains of the Hungarian Navy.

Orders came to send the DPs back to the Soviet zone. When this word got out to the Hungarians, they were filled with fear and despair.

At first they all thought that the good Americans who they had come to respect and know as friends would never allow this to happen. Most people in Europe had a total respect for America and what our nation stood for. It came as a great shock to them when it became known that the American soldiers had orders to ship them back, forcibly if necessary, in order to comply with an agreement Roosevelt made with the Russians at Yalta. The name of the implementation of this agreement was Operation Keelhaul. It turned out to be aptly named.

The people would come up to you on the street and ask in a pleading voice, "Why are you making us go back to the Reds?" We had no answer, only our sympathies. One day I was in Robbie Robinson's mayoral office when a Hungarian man came in and asked to be heard. His story was heart wrenching.

"Please, sir," he said in halting English, "I don't have much money or worldly goods, but you can have all that I own if you will not send me back to the East. You see, I was a newspaper editor in Budapest, and I wrote many editorials about the menace of Communism and the Red Russians. My name is high on their list to be executed. If you send me back it is to a certain death."

Robbie could only tell him that as soldiers we could only obey orders even if we did not agree with them. I stood there feeling sick and ashamed of an American policy that was against all that we held to be true. Here we had fought and won a war to overcome tyranny, and now we were actually helping the Soviets enslave a population.

Finally the day came when the trains arrived to take all the Hungarians back to the east. The people came down the cobblestone streets to the railroad yards where the lines of box cars awaited them.

All of the people lined up in the area around the tracks to be assembled and counted. This took a good amount of time and we soldiers moved among them saying goodbye and that we wished them well.

I remember one young mother with a baby. She was heating a bottle of milk by holding a lighted candle under it. I held the baby for awhile so she could get the bottle ready. I felt so sad as I thought of my sisters back in the States warming baby bottles on the gas range. What was going to happen to this mother and her child?

At last the waiting was over and the people had to climb into the open boxcars. Some were weeping, some shouted goodbye. The Hungarian soldiers, in their brown uniforms and soft peaked caps, looked helpless and forlorn.

After sharp piercing whistle blasts, the trains slowly pulled away. We stood there feeling helpless as the boxcars clunk-clunked past us on the rails. Finally they were gone. We turned and quietly walked up the road to Scharding. The American Army was not proud of itself on that day.

I remember riding in a jeep across the hills to pick up a lieutenant at Schardenberg. I was no longer asked to drive a jeep after my encounter with the barrel of the antitank gun. As we drove back with the lieutenant in the front seat, we talked about the new atomic bomb we had just heard had been dropped on Japan and what atomic energy meant for our future. The lieutenant said it would radically change all of our lives. In twenty years, he predicted there would be no such things as gas stations because everything would run on atomic power. Since we did not know any different, the driver and I agreed. We were more concerned about all of the jobs that would be lost if the gas stations closed. We began to wonder about what jobs there would be for us when we finally got home as we rode through the foggy mist over the hills of Austria.

I was given an added assignment, since I could speak some French, to be responsible for three French soldiers who somehow found their way into our part of Austria, two privates and one second lieutenant. Until headquarters learned what to do about them, I was their guide, interpreter, and companion.

Everywhere I went, they went along. Most of the GIs did not like the French. We were supposed to be allies, but the GIs liked the Germans and Austrians better. Possibly this was because of the difference they saw in the cleanliness of German homes versus the French homes they had been in. Also, not many Americans tried to learn to speak French because it sounded so foreign. Conversely, they did learn some German because many German words sounded so similar to English words. *Haus* is house, *strasse* is street, *milch* is milk, *Kaffee* is coffee, and so on.

Fellow GIs always razzed me about my "love for the French." We used to go for beer at Baumgardner's Cafe on the square in Scharding. I remember one Austrian girl, Jarmila Tscherpa, who spoke pretty good

English. When I was sitting at a table with my three charges, drinking big mugs of beer, she came in with some GIs, sat down at a table next to me, and yelled, "You! Always with the Frenchmen!" And her GI friends joined her in razzing me.

Because the GIs did not like the French generally, there were times that I had trouble getting our cooks to pass them through our chow line even though they were supposed to. I was always embarrassed and the three French soldiers were uncomfortable when the one cook would yell, "Why are we feeding the Frenchmen?"

The French *sous-lieutenant* was named Aimé Leroux and his home was in Paris. He was always such a gentleman and we became good friends. Later, when we left Austria to start our way home, he gave me a letter to his family, and when I got to Paris I visited them. Aimé and I thought we would keep in touch by writing to each other, but we never did.

One day I learned that the 87th Infantry Division was occupying the part of Germany just across the Inn River from Scharding. I decided to try to find my buddy Marty Agnew, who was transferred from our platoon to the 87th at Fort Jackson when we were shipped out, and he was in the hospital. I had his unit designation since we had written to each other a few times.

I got a jeep, crossed the big wooden bridge, and entered Germany. I got directions from some 87th troops on the road and drove to the village near Oberammergau, in Bavaria, where Marty's company was posted. I went up to the company CP and asked about him. One GI said, "I think he just left with a group to see a movie." I felt elated! He's alive! He made it too!

Just then a sergeant came out of the building and I mentioned that I had come to see my friend Agnew. He said, "Oh, he is *kaput.*"

I must have looked as stunned as I felt. "Sorry Mac," he continued, "he was shot right between the eyes as we were crossing the Elbe River. It was almost the last day of combat too. Don't worry though, I got the guy who shot him."

Some comfort, I thought, as if that mattered. The sergeant also told me that Marty kept saying every day, "I know that I'm going to get it. I just know it." Poor Marty, he used to wear such thick glasses that the YD GIs called him "Googs." He used to say that the sun reflecting off his glasses would make a fine target. I guess he was right.

That night, back at Scharding, I went for a long, solitary walk along the shore of the Inn River as the sun set over Bavaria and western Austria. I thought back to those days in Columbia, South Carolina, when I would go to town with my two buddies, Lambert Ciancaglini and Marty. Now they were both gone, and I was still alive. I asked myself, "Why did the good Lord take them and spare me? Did He have something else for me to do?" I thought that someday, somehow, I would write a book and tell people what war is like from the foot soldier's point of view.

When I got back to the schoolhouse, I wrote a letter to Marty's parents back at 288 Oliver Place in the Bronx. I promised to visit them sometime after I got back to the States, which I was able to do two years later. I corresponded with both his parents for years until they both died. His mother's name was Loretta.

Both Marty and Lambert were good solid men of real character. I could trust them to be honest in anything. In this life they were rare finds. I was so privileged to be able to have them as my friends. I always pray for them by name every Memorial Day Mass.

As part of my job as acting Special Service Officer, we got our little band together again to play for GI dances. We had a coronet, saxophone, drums, and piano. I was the band leader but I couldn't read a note of music or play any instrument. I would arrange for the dance location, publicity, and so on and then stand in front of the band, introduce each number, and direct. We had a lively group and were popular with GIs all over Upper Austria.

The leading personality of the musicians was Gabe, who was from New York. He made up our theme song "Matches" and the words, "Matches, matches, matches, some people strike 'em on the window, some strike 'em on the wall, I know a man who doesn't strike 'em at all. Matches, matches, M-A-T-C-H-E-S, I really mean it! M-A-T-C-H-E-S!!!"

The guy on the coronet could really belt out "*Stormy Weather*" and always got the most applause. Gabe pounded the piano and could make the greatest faces. Usually, at a break, he would ask the girls to gather around the bandstand and he would stand there with one leg across the back of a chair and tell a joke. The girls loved it, especially the American nurses. The skinny kid who played the drums knew just when to tap the drum for Gabe's punch line. TA-TA-TA-DUMMM.

One night we were asked to play for an officers'-nurses' dance in the Army Hospital at Passau. As we were carrying the instruments up the stairs of the hospital to the room for the dance, the nurse who was leading us got so excited. "Oh, real GIs! Great music at last!" she giggled. "We are so tired of Kraut bands who have no rhythm, no beat!"

It was a real party full of higher ranking officers and army nurses. No enlisted men were in sight except for our group. Then they put out a smorgasbord like I had never seen before. The officers all filled their plates and those of their nurse partners. I sauntered over to take a look. Then I picked up a plate and started to make my selections. I made a roast beef sandwich, spread on some mustard and made the mistake of reaching across the arm of a brigadier general to get the pickles. He turned and looked down his nose at me with some annoyance and I smiled and said, "Great party, sir! Hope you are enjoying it." He turned away without speaking, and I went back to my area to eat my sandwich.

My attitude toward the war was to pay respect to all higher authority and to obey the rules. However, now that the war was over, and we were all citizen soldiers just awaiting our turn to go back to civilian life, I thought a party was a party.

The next morning I was called into Captain Timm's office at the Gold Cross Hotel, and he told me that in the future I would stay in my place and not participate in any parties where the band played, and particularly not touch any food. I respectfully asked to be relieved of my assignment as the acting SSO and to return to my AT squad. Captain Timms picked up the phone and got connected to regimental headquarters and the officer who had passed the reprimand on to him from the general no doubt.

"Sir, PFC Courtney wants to be relieved of his job as SSO and go back to his squad. Yes, Sir. Just a moment, Sir." He turned to me, "The colonel wants to know if you will reconsider and stay on?" I was amazed that I was not ordered to stay on but I said, "No, Sir."

"No, Sir, his mind is made up. He wants to return to his squad. Yes, Sir, I will try to find a replacement," and he hung up.

"O.K. Courtney. You can report back to your platoon and move to the company barracks in the old schoolhouse."

I saluted and left.

As I walked back to get my gear out of the gray stone school building to move to the south Scharding location, I said to myself, "Well, dum-dum. Now you've done it. You have lost your freedom to move around at will. Now you will have to go on guard duty! Big deal!"

When I got to the third floor of the school building the guys were all gathered around for a dice game on the floor. We had just gotten paid for the first time in two months, so everyone had schillings to burn. I sat on my bunk and dropped ten dollars worth of schillings on the floor. Bennett rolled eleven. "Shoot all or any part of it," he laughed. I dropped ten dollars more. He rolled seven! I turned to all the other guys who were also dropping ten dollars each time. "He can't do that again!" I said, and we all dropped ten more dollars on the floor. Bennett had this maddening laugh as he rolled seven! We all groaned.

Joe Lieb came up the stairs and into the room and surveyed the crowd and the pile of schilling notes in the center of the floor. "Look at this Joe!" Bennett laughed. "Can you believe this? Shoot all or any part of it," he laughed. We all dropped our ten dollars again and Bennett rolled seven! Groans mixed with Bennett's loud laughter as I left the game and the room. I had just shot two months pay. As I hiked down the street carrying my barracks bag, I thought to myself, "Kid, this has not been your day."

When I checked into my squad in the yellow stucco schoolhouse, I heard them complain of the food, always the same stuff, lots of powdered eggs and canned meat. I suggested that some of us ought to go hunting for game.

The next morning Larry Choiniere and I got Joe Lieb to drive us out to the hills east of Scharding. We took German shotguns along to hunt for quail. We saw a few but they got away before we could shoot. I almost shot Larry when the trigger of my shotgun caught on a tree branch and fired a burst of pellets just to his left as we crossed a ditch. For the rest of the day all we could see were deer everywhere. We decided to come back the next day armed with .30 caliber carbines.

The next day we drove back to the same area and all we saw all day were quail. We started to shoot bottles and cans just for practice. We were driving home when I spotted three deer in a field just down the hill from us. Joe and Larry were out of ammo and I was down to three rounds. The deer sensed us and started to run across the meadow to get into the woods.

I lined up my sights on the leader, fired, and missed as he got into the woods. I aimed at the second deer and fired. I missed again as he ran away. With my last round I took aim at the last deer, led him a little, and fired. He dropped, shot in the head.

We dragged the deer back to the jeep and put him on the hood. An Austrian boy about fourteen years old came along the road and offered to clean the deer for us, so we accepted. He pulled out his knife and did a quick and efficient job. We rewarded him with some cigarettes, which had become common currency.

We wound down out of the hills proud of our kill and were talking about how much our fellow GIs would enjoy the venison we brought.

As we turned the corner of the fence that surrounded the school, we were surprised to see nineteen deer hung in a row on the iron fence. Seems like other soldiers had the same idea about hunting fresh meat. We ate venison for weeks and got sick of it. By the way, the Austrian deer we shot were only about as big as police dogs.

While I was still regarded as the kid by many older GIs, I had seniority since I had been in the YD longer than the replacements. Also, I knew many guys in our battalion and lots of them knew me. It had been announced that passes were going to be issued for ten-day trips to Paris, Brussels, London, or Dublin. The trip would be by air and all expenses paid for food and lodging.

Since these passes were going to be issued every ten days, a few per each battalion, on a seniority basis, I thought I had a good chance of getting one. When I talked to the first sergeant about going to Ireland, he told me you could only go to Ireland if you could prove you had relatives there. It was a rule of the Irish government so they would not be overrun with Yankee soldiers. Also, you could only take thirty-five dollars into Ireland.

I had written home weeks before and my mother had sent me our cousin's address in Dublin. I had turned over the letter to Sergeant McKittrick and he put my name on the list.

Many weeks passed and I did not hear anything about getting one of those passes. We all heard rumors that troops were being rotated home. We had even seen pictures in magazines of shiploads of GIs being welcomed into New York Harbor with bands and girls blowing kisses from tugboats.

I began to tell myself that I would soon be going home, and I had not yet seen any sights of Europe. So, one fine morning I hitched a ride in a jeep to the city of Linz. I went along with Doc, of our old battalion patrol group, whom I had known from the Bulge and Saarlautern. I never knew Doc's last name or where he got the nickname "Doc." Fifty years later I learned from Bill Houle, also a member of the patrol group, that Doc's name was Leon Farmilant and his home was Chicago.

Doc was quite an operator. He had set up a business on the side and had other GI partners in towns all over Upper Austria. Each morning he would go to the 3rd Battalion signal center and get the operator to hook up phone connections to his buddies who were waiting at their company CPs to receive his call. He would ask how the market was for soap in Passau, typewriters in Linz, or shoes in Bad Schallerbach.

Then he would direct his "operator" partners where to deliver the needed products and collect the money. I was amazed at the business acumen of this entrepreneur. He was a little, soft-spoken, unassuming fellow, but I'll bet he went home rich and must be running some enterprise in the States.

Doc was on his way to pick up a load of typewriters at Linz, so on an impulse I got in the jeep with him. On the way there, Doc was telling the driver about the day at Saarlautern when the two of us sauntered back across the bridge and had German machine gun bullets sprayed into the puddles by our feet. We all laughed about it.

When we arrived in Linz, which is a sizable city, Doc showed me a building where they provided meals and sleeping cots for transient soldiers. I had supper there as Doc headed back to Scharding with his load of typewriters. I was excited to see streetcars running and hear their bells ringing. It brought back memories of the Logan Valley Streetcar Company back home.

At the desk of the GI hotel, I saw a sign advertising a play in a local theater. It said tickets were available to GIs, so I asked for one. When I got to the theater, only a few blocks away, I learned that my ticket was for a box seat. I felt like a big dealer sitting up there. If only my dad could see me now!

There was an Austrian couple in the same box, and they greeted me warmly and I responded with a few words of German. The play turned out to be a comedy and I could not keep up with all the German language spoken so when everyone else laughed I laughed too. This impressed my box mates as they said *"Ach so! Du kannst gut Deutsch verstehen!"* (Ah, so you can understand German.) I replied, *"Nicht viel aber genug."* (Not much, but enough.) I strolled back to the GI hotel very pleased with the evening.

At breakfast the next morning, I heard a group of GIs talking about a train they had to catch. Seems they were a group that was going on a tour of the Alps. So I walked along with their group to the railroad station, and there they were met by the tour leader who I recognized as a GI from M Company.

I did not know his name and he did not know mine, however, we remembered each other from days on the line in combat. He told me the group was going to Salzburg and Berchtesgaden. I asked if I could be included in the group, and he said yes. Once more it paid to be an old YD man.

It was a beautiful train. The coaches were blue and we sat on cushioned seats as we rolled southward across Austria. At lunch we went into a real dining car and sat at tables where we were served by civilians.

Each man was served a large slice of ham on a real china plate. We felt like royalty. As we were starting to eat our meal, the train arrived in the town of Wels and stopped in the railroad yards. Right outside our windows we could see about one hundred German POWs working on the tracks. They stopped working to look at us, and the guy seated next to me dug his fork into his ham slice and held it up to the window for the Germans to see and yelled, "Yeah! And it's good too!" The POWs looked at us with envy.

Finally we arrived in Salzburg, which is a beautiful city nestled at the base of several mountains. We were loaded onto a large bus that ran on steam from a huge wood-burning kettle. It wheezed and chugged and did not go very fast, but it struggled along.

As we moved along, enthralled by the beautiful buildings and the quaintness of Salzburg, we could see evidence of the Big Red One (the 1st Infantry Division) all over town. This is where they ended up at the end of the war. I remember one big stone building had a new sign across the front that read "II Corps Playhouse."

The bus started to climb through the mountains, and we all wondered if it had enough power to make it, but it did. We came to another valley and the more beautiful village of Berchtesgaden. Then the bus really started to wheeze as it climbed up the mountain to the Berghof, Hitler's home. We all got out there and were met by a German tour guide who started in a loud voice, speaking English, to describe all the big homes on the mountain.

We walked past Hermann Goering's house but did not go in as we all wanted to use the time to see Hitler's house. As we walked up the hill we came to the flight of stone steps that led up to Hitler's front door. I stopped and gazed up at the house and the big picture window at the front. So this was it!

I remembered sitting in a movie theater back home in 1938 when I was only thirteen years old. It was a Movietone newsreel showing Neville Chamberlain going up these same steps and Adolf Hitler coming down the steps to greet him.

What must Chamberlain have been thinking as he mounted those steps? Hitler got Chamberlain inside where he scared him so badly that later on, in Munich, he willingly signed a paper giving Czechoslovakia to Germany, which led to the beginning of World War II.

And now here was Pfc. Courtney walking up the same steps after helping to win the war against Hitler and his Nazi cronies. No movie cameras were around to record this visit, but I will always remember how I felt that day, August 19, 1945.

Inside, the house was a wreck. The men of the 101st Airborne who captured the place destroyed or carried off all the furnishings and left their names and home towns written all over the plaster walls. The picture window glass was all knocked out of the big window in the front living room.

I put one foot up on the window sill as I stood there taking in the gorgeous view of the valley and the surrounding mountain peaks. So this is where Hitler stood and looked out over Europe and said, "All this is mine!"

Back when I was in high school, we used to walk across the railroad tracks on a footbridge, and I remember the day we saw trainloads of German POWs from the Afrika Korps pass by on their way to POW camps. It seemed then that Hitler had a grip on Europe that maybe no one could ever break. He must have been very confident then to look out this window and sneer at any thought of the Americans' trying to liberate Europe.

I was standing there musing about all this when someone tapped me on the shoulder and I heard a voice say, "Aren't you Dick Courtney?" I turned around and there stood Joe Abu, a GI from Michigan who went through basic training with me back at Camp Croft in Spartanburg, South Carolina. I said, "Imagine this, meeting again in Hitler's living room!"

Joe and I renewed our acquaintance and brought each other up to date on the other guys we knew about. We spent the rest of the afternoon together but never thought to exchange home addresses. In those days all GIs lived for the day. Something we learned during combat.

At the very peak of the mountain there was a smaller house called the Eagle's Nest. There was an elevator built into the mountain to reach the house. We heard that the elevator was for officers only and that enlisted men, if they wanted to go up to the Eagle's Nest, had to walk up on a precarious footpath to the top. We decided not to go.

Later on I read in the *Stars and Stripes* that General Eisenhower had visited the area, saw the sign which read "Officers Only," and had given orders to get rid of the sign. Bill Mauldin must have had this in mind when he drew the cartoon showing two officers standing at a lookout admiring the view of a sunset on top of mountain peaks. The caption under the cartoon read, "Beautiful! Is there one for the enlisted men?"

The same big square bus brought us down the mountain to Berchtesgaden where we went into a beautiful lodge used as a USO club. I ate a sandwich and drank a stein of good German beer and then sat in the lobby to listen to a German man play a big grand piano. I could have stayed and listened to him all night as he played such beautiful music, and the sun was setting behind the Alpine peaks, which I could see through the large, two-story-high glass window.

The bus was ready to go, so we loaded up for the trip back to Salzburg. The group from the train had tickets to attend the Vienna Boy's Choir concert in the Mozarteum. My pal from M Company came up with a ticket for me, so I sat right in the center of the main floor. We were all waiting for the curtain to go up when there was a stir in the middle box section to our right. We all looked up to see Soviet Marshal Georgi Zhukov and American General Mark Clark take their seats. The audience of mostly GIs gave them a rousing round of applause. I recognized Zhukov by his chunky build and his short crewcut. We had all seen pictures of General Clark who was now commander of USFA, United States Forces in Austria. He had formerly commanded the US Fifth Army in Italy. Both officers nodded their greeting and acceptance of the applause, but neither one smiled, stood up, or waved. I thought Zhukov was trying to look stoic and Clark was trying to emulate him.

It was an enjoyable performance as those boys had the sweetest voices. I thought I was really in high society now to hear the world-famed Vienna Boy's Choir in person and be seated in the same theater with two army commanders. As Lieutenant Deviese said back in the cellar at Sarre Union in Alsace-Lorraine, "It is the changing fortunes of a soldier's life."

The biggest applause came when they announced a special number for the American soldiers and sang "Yankee Doodle."

We were all humming the tunes as we came outside and headed for the train that took us back to Linz. I found my way back to the GI hotel and sacked out for the night.

The next morning I got a ride in a jeep going to Scharding. As I got out of the jeep in front of our company CP in the yellow schoolhouse, I ran into Bernie McKittrick, who was now the company first sergeant. "Courtney! Where have you been? We've been looking everywhere for you this weekend. Your pass to Ireland came through and since we couldn't find you, I gave it to Art Schwartz and he went to London."

I mumbled something about being away and went on into the barracks. Wow! I had a great trip, but I could have gone to Ireland and even had my first plane ride. Is this what they mean by the luck of the Irish?

10

A Slow Train Across Germany to Reims and Paris

As the train slowly crept out of Austria, we all were punching each other and laughing. Joe Puchalski, my friend from Scranton, Pennysylvania, gave me a big Polish grin and said, "Well, Court, we are on our way at last! It can't come too soon for me. I am anxious to get home to my wife Sue and son Vince."

As I looked around the boxcar, I remembered that beautiful, blue train I had ridden from Linz to Salzburg. This was just the opposite. We were packed into cattle cars about twenty men to a car. All we had with us were light packs with a raincoat, one blanket, shelter half, canteen, and messkit.

The days were warm and sunny but the nights were cold. We learned to huddle close together to sleep on the wooden floor with our blanket and shelter half over us. Of course, we had no latrines in the boxcars and relief was at the mercy of the engineer—when he chose to stop the train. This got to be hilarious as GIs desperate for relief would jump off as soon as the train stopped and run to the nearest ditch. Since we had no idea of how soon the train would go forward again, we did not know if we had one minute or half an hour.

Men were often caught halfway finished when the train started to go again and had to hobble back to the cars and often be pulled aboard by the hands of GI buddies inside the car. We all yelled, "Typical Army SNAFU! Can't someone set up a signal when the train will be stopped for awhile? Does this take a lot of intelligence?"

By the second day, someone had gotten a message to the railroad engineer. When the train stopped, if it was going to be ten minutes or longer, a wooden pole with a red cloth attached was hung out from the engine cab. When the whistle blew and the red flag was pulled back into the steam engine cab, you had better run and crawl back into your boxcar.

Maybe it was because we were anxious to keep moving westward and toward home, but this seemed to be the slowest train ever and it also had many stops. We waited at every side track for other, faster trains to whiz by. On the second night, we were stopped in a railroad yard in a German town when a beautiful, blue German train stopped alongside us. It was a coach train full of German soldiers, most of them wounded, on their way to Berlin.

I didn't know how it got started, but soon the Germans who could speak English were taunting the Americans about the dirty boxcars they were riding while the Germans were in beautiful coaches. GIs soon lashed back with caustic blasts. "Wait until you get home to four walls and a chimney in Berlin, Kraut!" "Your girlfriend is sleeping with a Russian, Heinz!"

One German right across from me yelled, "I grew up in Baltimore. We beat the crap out of you! Americans can't fight!"

I yelled back, "Sit down in your wheelchair, you cripple! Who won the war? We did!"

Fortunately, this brief exchange between the two armies was ended as the German troop train pulled out.

In the morning sunshine, we slowly passed through the city of Stuttgart, and I remember how destroyed the place looked.

The cathedral of Stuttgart stood up very proudly across the river as the train curved in an arc that gave us a sweeping view of the city. I had hoped to come back and see the inside of that cathedral some day.

Later on we came to a high, level bridge of stone arches where workers were repairing wartime damage to the structure. I was scared that the bridge would soon collapse before our train got across. The German workers looked as if they hoped it would as they could see we were an American Army train. We sat on the floor of the boxcar with our legs dangling out of the side door as we looked down at the river far below.

As we slowly chugged and chugged across Germany, the people from the adjacent towns would come out to see what they could trade with the GIs. The Germans wanted woolen clothing and GIs traded their shirts, sweaters, and some even their pants for jars of chicken, pickles, and tubs of beer. One guy was down to his raincoat and boots when we finally ended the trip.

I remember how beautiful it was around Heidelberg and Karlsruhe. These were ancient cities of learning and the buildings were so well designed and reflected their antiquity. We wished the train had stopped there at meal time so that we could explore more. It was not to be, but we drank in all the beauty we could see from the boxcar door.

Early in the evening we crossed the border from Germany to France. Nobody had to tell us we were in France as we saw the first French village. It looked so drab and dirty compared to the clean buildings in German villages.

Late that night the train stopped near Strasbourg, France. We were fed from local GI kitchens along the route of our train. They would set up a food serving line of pans and kettles resting on top of benches. We would wash our mess kits by dipping them into garbage cans full of hot water heated by a gas heater unit placed inside the can. There would be three such cans: one to dip first, second for soapy water, third had boiling clear water for rinse.

After we got our meal and stood around or found a log to sit on while we ate, we then went back through the three cans to clean our mess kit again. On the exit trip there was another can into which we spilled our leftover food. Usually there would be a dozen or so kids or old folks around this can who tried to get your garbage before you knocked it into the can.

All the GIs tried to give their food to the little kids but sometimes the adults would shoulder the kids out of their way and hold out their cans. Very often both kids and the older folks would dip their cans right into the trash can in order to get something to eat. We got used to seeing this all over Europe. A lot of guys saved half their meal to give to the hungry civilians.

Next morning we finally chugged into Reims and out to a tent city called Camp Pittsburgh. We learned that temporary tent sites were set up to house the troops enroute to embarkation ports. Some of the camps were named Camp Lucky Strike, Camp Camel, and so forth. Since a lot of us were Pennsylvanians we were glad to be in Camp Pittsburgh.

We were glad to get off the 40 X 8 boxcars and get into the pyramidal tents. As soon as we got located, we headed for the tent showers. It felt so good to be clean again.

Camp Pittsburgh was a holding area as troops were warehoused until a ship was available to rotate them back to the U.S. We had no guard duty nor formations. All we had to do was eat, read books, write letters, and watch old movies shown in the Quonset hut.

A Quonset hut was a building made by bolting curved, metal corrugated panels together to form what looked like a culvert. There were end panels and a door but no heat—at least in these huts.

Somehow there was a shortage of light bulbs. Each tent had one light bulb hanging from the center post. GIs who did not have a bulb in their tent would go and steal one from some other tent while the occupants were away. To protect their tent, each squad had to set up a guard roster to make sure that someone was in the tent at all times to guard the precious bulb.

One day we were in the Quonset theater watching a movie when the film broke. The operator yelled for someone to turn on the top light so he could repair the film. Nobody could turn on a light since some GI had lifted the light bulb while it was dark and the movie was on.

The operator screamed to have the bulb put back or else there would be no movie. This brought a roar from the GI audience who wanted to see the movie. "Put the bulb back!" they yelled in unison. The anger kept rising as the GIs shouted louder. However, by now the bulb thief did not dare reveal his identity. After much jostling and yelling, we all piled out of the Quonset hut. No more movies that day. Everyone was mad.

We could get afternoon passes to Reims and ride the shuttle bus into town. I went as often as I could and really got to know the town. Of course the top attraction for me was the beautiful cathedral of Reims. I had often seen pictures and heard about its beauty.

We had a Mass for our troops in the cathedral and discovered that only the front part of the church had wooden chairs with attached kneelers on the back. Most of the latecomers had to stand on the concrete floor.

Once again, being an "old-timer" with the outfit paid off as I was able to get a three-day pass to Paris. About ten of us were loaded into the back of a $2^1/2$-ton Army truck and driven to Paris where we arrived right at the end of a big French parade. It was November 11th, 1945, Armistice Day.

Our truck stopped for the parade and for the first time saw a French military band on horseback, which was quite unusual to see.

At the end of the parade came Gen. Charles de Gaulle, who rode all by himself in the third seat of an open limousene. There was a driver and a uniformed guard in the front seat and the second seat was empty. DeGaulle sat in the middle of the back seat and held his arms out like a ballerina taking a bow.

I had passed DeGaulle on a street in Metz and had saluted him then, so I saluted him now when he looked in our direction and he returned my salute. His car turned away from the parade then and drove across the plaza to the Presidential Palace, which was a fancy big home surrounded by a high, wrought-iron fence. I learned later that evening that he was now the Provisional President of France.

He was always known as a stubborn, bullheaded man, yet he always stood up for France, and the French people loved him.

After we drove through the after-parade traffic, we arrived at the front door of our hotel. It was the Hotel Moderne, temporarily renamed the Transatlantic Club for the American military.

We eagerly went up to see our rooms. I was given room number 266 on the second floor. I remember the number even to this day as I would proudly tell the key clerk on our floor, *"le nombre deux cent soixante-six"* and his eyes would light up.

"Ah! Vous parlais Français!"

I had a large room all to myself with a double bed and private bath. The whole room was decorated in dark red, even the heavy drapes on the windows. "Ah! The changing fortunes of a soldier's life," I told myself.

We ate supper in a gorgeous, big dining room with glass chandeliers. The lobby had deep red carpet, and the stairs up to the balcony had a dark red pattern. The trimming was all gold or brass. If mother and dad could only see their boy Dick now! I sat down and wrote a letter and described the hotel to them. After that I went for a walk out front on the boulevard with another GI to sell some cigarettes to raise some money. It took only a few minutes until a little man came up behind us and said, "Perhaps you have cigarettes to sell?" in French-accented English. In a few minutes I had the equivalent of forty dollars in French francs. French money was made like tissue paper, and you had to be careful not to tear it. We were used to heavy paper Austrian schillings and German marks.

I decided to buy a ticket on a tour bus for sixty francs, which took me all over Paris at night and gave me a general idea of the layout of the city.

The next day I set out to locate the military office where Ted Holt was located. Ted was in our AT squad in Alsace-Lorraine and had gotten hurt falling off the gun trails near Metz, where he was evacuated. He had written to give me his Army address and to tell me that he had married a Parisian girl.

When I located his office, I learned that he was offduty for the day, but they gave me his apartment address. After awhile I found it and knocked on the door. Ted looked surprised as he saw me standing there when he opened the door. He had not known whether I survived the war or not. He led me into a living room to meet his wife, who was quite a looker. She had blond hair in a high, bouffant style and big green eyes.

After we talked for awhile they decided to give me a tour of Paris. We went first to Notre-Dame, which I thought was very dull and dark inside. In fact, all of Paris was drab and sooty. I heard later the French sand blasted the stone buildings back to their original beauty about 1952.

We walked around the downtown area, and they showed me the Church of the Madeleine where they had been married and also the Opéra.

Of all the places Ted and his wife showed me, I enjoyed Sacré Coeur the best. The Basilica of the Sacred Heart is a beautiful, soft domed, white stone building at the top of an incline on Montmartre hill. It was so impressive.

We went inside the crypt where there was a glass case that held a hanging white cloth with the bloody face of Christ on it. They called it Veronica's cloth, but it had to be a copy. It sure did hold my attention though.

Ted and "Honey," as he called his wife, enjoyed the inclined car ride up to the church. She nestled against him and said they were still on their honeymoon, so when we got back to center city area I took my leave of them. Ted said, "Wait until the folks in Boston see her!" I agreed with him.

I decided then to try to find the home of my friend, Aimé Leroux, the French lieutenant I looked after in Austria. I stopped a gendarme and asked him where I could find:

6, rue de Debolyenne
Deuxième Arrondisement
Paris

He gave me good directions and I was able to find my way. When I got to the number, it was a combination home and neighborhood bar. When I introduced myself and showed them the letter Aimé had given me to give to them, they took me into the bar and brought out some wine. We talked about Aimé and Austria and they asked if I knew when Aimé was coming home, which I didn't.

They were very reserved people and not as warm and friendly as Aimé. Although Aimé, in his letter, asked them to give me two bottles of champagne to take home and put the cost on his bill, they made no reference to it, so neither did I. After about an hour or so I said, "*Au revoir*" and left.

The next morning I walked alone down the Champs-Elysées to the Arc de Triomphe. The Arch of Triumph is a huge stone monument that sits in the middle of a large, busy traffic circle. I could see a flame coming up in the center of the arch, so I decided to walk out and take a closer look.

I had quite a time dodging all the cars and taxi cabs that roared around the circle. Finally I stood under the arch to see the flame up close and the big tricolor French flag which hung inside the arch.

About this time a French police car swung alongside the arch, and an agitated gendarme waved me to get out of there. Apparently you are only to look at the arch from the distant sidewalk. It is sacred ground under the arch. I learned that, out of respect, even the German army marched around the arch in 1940 as they entered Paris.

When I got back to the safety of the sidewalk on the Champs-Elysées, I stood looking in a store window at some pictures that were taken of the Armistice Day parade. A smiling French soldier came up to me and pointed out, very proudly, that the man in the photograph leading the whole parade was him!

I shook hands and congratulated him. His name was E. Tetoka A Tane and his home was, Ile de Takaroa, Tuamotou, Par E.F.O. Papeete, Tahiti. He was very friendly and offered to trade hats with me, but I declined as I did not want to show up to Camp Pittsburgh wearing a blue beret with a white tassel, which was his uniform hat. He was a French Territorial Army soldier.

On the way back to the hotel, I stopped in a store and bought some face powder which I sent home to my three sisters. Later they told me it was the lightest powder they had ever used.

I also stopped to buy a bottle of cognac to take back to my squad at Reims. It had become the custom that anyone who went away on a pass should bring back a bottle.

With the time I had left, I strolled along the wide sidewalks of the Champs and admired the girls. They were very different from the girls of Austria and Germany. Very chic. High bouffant hairdos and snazzy clothes. They walked fast too.

Although I had taken pictures around Paris I found I had one shot left to take on my roll of film so I picked out an especially attractive, well-dressed girl who was walking by and asked her, *"S'il vous plait. Puis je prendre votre foto?"*

She smiled, stopped, said *"Oui"* and I took her picture. I still have the photo.

It was a misty, cloudy November afternoon as our truck pulled away, and we waved goodbye to the Eiffel Tower. So now, I had seen Paris. *Au Revoir!*

11

Marseilles, the Stormy Atlantic Ocean, New York, Fort Dix, Indiantown Gap, and Home

WHEN I GOT BACK TO MY SQUAD AT CAMP PITTSBURGH, they all gathered around and made short work of the bottle of cognac I had brought. Some of the guys laughed and jeered when they learned that I did not go to the Place Pigalle or the Folies Bergère. "You wasted your pass," they sneered.

One day, to our surprise, the whole 104th Regiment was formed by companies and marched out to the center of a big field next to the camp. We were all rusty in marching and there were many shouts from the officers to "straighten up that line," "get in step," "look sharp."

When we were finally assembled in parade formation, a French band appeared on the scene and French officers who stood opposite our formation.

After some shouted commands in French and a roll of the drums by the band, our regimental commander, Col. Ralph Pallidino, and a few of his staff officers marched forward and halted a few paces in front of the French officers.

The French officer in charge then stepped up to our colonel and kissed him on both cheeks and rendered a hand salute. His staff officers then stepped forward and did the same hugging and kissing routine on Colonel Pallidino's staff officers.

Then the senior French officer read out loud, in French, from a long paper. We learned later that our regiment was being decorated with the Croix de Guerre for our action in liberating the French province of Alsace-Lorraine.

After the officer read the notice, which we could not understand, they all saluted and Colonel Pallidino and his staff marched back to join the regiment. All through our ranks you could hear GIs muttering, "If those Frenchies try to hug or kiss me I will slug them!" Others would join in with, "Yeah, Me too!"

The band started to play a snappy tune, and we received shouted orders to "Pass in review!" By companies, the whole regiment marched past the reviewing stand where the French officers saluted as we were given "Eyes, right!" then "Ready, front!"

We all then marched back to our company area where we stood at attention until each man was given a copy of the Croix de Guerre citation. Our company commander shouted, "Each man will receive his own Fourragère de la Croix de Guerre in the next few days. Dismissed!"

GIs, with typical Army humor, irreverently shouted, "How many points is this French medal worth sir?" This was followed by loud guffaws and general laughter. No one was impressed with the medal parade, but all agreed that it did relieve the boredom for awhile.

That night at chow we all noticed that Captain Timm was wearing his new decoration. The fourragère of the Croix de Guerre (Cross of War) decoration is a green and red braided rope that loops over your left shoulder and fastens on to the epaulet button of the dress uniform. At the end of the rope there is a metal piece about two inches long that resembles a cannon barrel. In a few days we each received a "rope" as we called it and had fun figuring out how to put them on. Although we kidded a lot about the decoration, it sure did dress up our uniforms.

Just when we began to think we would be stuck here forever, a train arrived on the siding, and we were crammed into those 40 X 8 boxcars again. We were told only that we were headed for Marseilles, the port on the Mediterranean.

It was cold as we chugged slowly through the south of France. I remember when we came to another high arched stone bridge, which looked like it had been built by the Romans. It too had sustained some war damage, and there was a French crew of workers repairing it. We all held our breath as we wobbled over the span, but we finally did make it across.

At last the engine chugged to a stop. We were there. We all hopped off our boxcars eager to see the city of Marseilles. But where was it?

We were out in the country and walked until we came to another tent city. This one was not named as the cigarette camps were at Reims. It had no name.

Later we found out that we were on a plateau above Marseilles and the area was called Plain de Cuques. Once more we were herded into tents and instinctively we all checked to see if our tent had a light bulb.

We settled down to day after day of boredom again. We got some newspapers and magazines that showed pictures of American ships arriving in New York harbor with bands playing and girls waving. I remember one picture in *Life* magazine showing a GI being held over the side of a ship by his ankles to kiss a girl who was standing on the deck of a tugboat.

All the guys were saying, "By the time we ever get to New York the bands and girls will all have gone home and the paint on the Welcome Home signs will be faded and peeling."

Finally, one day we lined up to be paid, in French money. We were told that our cash would all be converted into American dollars on the pier the next day. The reason given was that they did not want the American greenbacks to go out into the French economy where they went for a premium.

Before supper time we received copies of the Army information sheet, a half page of paper typed with the current news, commonly referred to by the GIs as the "poop sheet." We eagerly read the list of ships in the harbor and when they would be sailing for the United States. We learned that the 104th Regiment of the 26th Division would sail the next day, December 15th, on the SS *Rock Hill Victory*.

The poop sheet also reported that during a heavy storm recently, one ship was blown across the harbor and rammed a hole in the side of another ship. We all laughed, and remarked, "Some poor guys will have to wait until they fix the hole in their ship. At least we know we have a ship assigned and ready to leave tomorrow." The poop sheet did not mention the name of the damaged vessel.

After supper I counted up my money and found I had the equivalent of seventy U.S. dollars in "toilet paper" French money, as the GIs called it. I said to myself, "This is it. Tomorrow I can go home to an outhouse or a castle. I put ten dollars worth of French money in my pocket, one piece of paper, I think it was 1,000 francs. No matter what happens tonight, I won't gamble that money as I want to buy things on the ship.

Bravely and confidently, I left my tent and walked down the row of tents until I could hear a dice game. I went into the tent and entered the fray. It only took about an hour until I slowly walked back to my tent broke, except for the ten dollars in my hip pocket.

The next day was a bright sunny, warm day and with our duffle bags we were loaded on semi-trailer trucks. We all stood up as we rode down the switchbacks from the plateau to the city of Marseilles below us.

I began to be a little apprehensive when I first caught sight of our little GI driver with an Army sweater and a small wool knit cap as his uniform. This began to grow into fear as he gunned his engine and roared away and we all fell against each other. We came to the top of the mountain and saw the city and the Mediterranean Sea below us as all the GIs shouted to "Slow down you S.O.B.!"

This had no effect on our little Barney Oldfield as he sailed down the mountain at full speed. He barely touched his air brakes as we hit the first turn and swung around to the opposite direction as we all piled up on the floor of the trailer.

"Dear God, No," I prayed, "Don't let us die here!" as we slammed back and forth on the switchbacks until we arrived to a jerky stop on the end of a pier. As we piled off the trailer, guys were screaming at the pint-size driver in his baggy fatigue pants. "Where did you learn to drive, Meathead?"

He was not fazed a bit. He grinned and yelled back, "That's nothing. You should be along when the brakes are out of air!"

As we tried to recover our composure after the wild roller-coaster ride, we looked up to see *Rock Hill Victory* painted on this rusty ship. Then we saw it, and we all gasped! There was a giant hole in the side of the ship about twenty feet square, and it was filled with concrete as a patch! Concrete!

Boy did a big howl go up against the French then. Don't these Frenchies know how to weld metal onto metal? Who ever heard of a concrete patch for an ocean-going ship?

Once more I thought about the changing fortunes of a soldier's life. None of us would have set foot on that ship if we had the choice. But we didn't, so we slowly inched forward along the pier until we came to a table where our company commander sat with a pile of American dollars. Boy did they look beautiful after all this time of seeing only funny money.

Each man ahead of me received a big handful as he traded in his French tissue paper. Finally I stood there, sheepishly, as I handed over my one piece of paper. The captain shouted, "Courtney! What happened to you?"

"They didn't roll right for me, sir," I replied, as I moved on down the line.

This time we did go up a real gangplank, single file with our duffle bags over our shoulders. We had turned in all of our gear except our clothing. I had two German dress bayonets and a P-38 pistol in my bag. There was no band or pretty French girls to see us off. The pier was deserted except for two old dock workers who looked like they would fall asleep at any moment.

We went down in the hold and located a hammock and pipe frame. This time we were not up on B deck. I don't think they even had a B deck on this ship. I was up about four high on the bunk pipe frame. As soon as I stowed my bag I headed up the ladder to go out on the narrow deck. This was a real ladder which ran straight up, not a set of stairs like we had on the USS *Argentina*.

As I stood there leaning on the rail, I looked out on the cup of mountains that surrounded the harbor. "So long France and so long Europe," I thought.

We all lined the rail eager to get going. The ship's engines were not even started. What was the holdup now? We were all aboard. Even the gangplank had been pulled up. "What is the delay?" I asked a ship's crewman who was standing next to me.

"We're waiting for the pilot to guide us out of the harbor," he said. He had such a heavy British accent that I asked him if this was an English ship. "No, American," he assured me.

Looking down at the pier, I could see a tall, old Frenchman wearing black boots and a black beret. He finally ambled up to the side of the ship and yelled up to the crew. In a minute the crew dropped a rope ladder over the side and the old man slowly pulled himself up. We all wondered why they did not lower the gangplank, but that was up to the seamen and their ways I guess.

Finally we heard a hum as the engines throbbed to life. I did not realize that they would be so loud. Still we did not move. We looked over the side to see what the hold up was now. There they were, the two sleepy-head dock workers ever so slowly ambling up the pier toward the bow. When they reached a stanchion, they ever so slowly, and with seemingly great effort, pulled the hawser loose and let it fall into the water to be pulled into the ship.

A cheer went up from the GIs, which quickly died as the two slowly started to walk toward the hawser tied to the pier at the stern of the ship. Guys were yelling at them to hurry up as we wanted to get home. The more the guys yelled, the slower the Frenchies walked.

They were enjoying themselves and were in no hurry. I thought back to the three Frenchmen in that little round boat on our first day in Cherbourg harbor.

"Ah!" I said to myself. What a great opening scene for the book I planned to write as soon as I could get a pen and paper on board. I still had the notes I had kept as we crossed Europe in combat.

As I watched the Frenchmen walk slowly down the pier toward the stern, I said to myself, "This rope is our last tie to the Old World. When those workers finally toss the line back to the ship we will be free. Free of Europe and the old ways. We had come, done our duty, so now we could go home and be just plain Americans once more."

I was thinking this as the ship floated free of the pier and we slid out into the channel. I used my last 127V film to take pictures of the harbor as we left.

In time we were out on the blue Mediterranean and the sun was just beginning to sink like a big globe fire into the water on the horizon. A little breeze had sprung up. I thought we would have a delightful cruise. Just then the GI in front of me along the port rail, who must have had a weak stomach, turned with his mouth open and it seemed like a stream of scrambled eggs flew out into the air. I ducked as if a mortar shell was landing, but the guy behind me caught the full menu. What a mess! The language was, of course, unprintable. We had not even hit any waves yet.

We all swung loose as we slept in our hammocks that night, perhaps dreaming, as we were now on our final leg home. I awoke before dawn and Joe Puchalski and I climbed up on deck to see the shores of Morocco, North Africa, as we passed the Rock of Gibraltar.

We stood out to sea now heading into black thunderclouds on the North Atlantic. Little did we realize that those thunderclouds were part of a storm that would be with us for ten days and ten nights, all the way to Christmas.

The storm burst upon us and the ship tossed and turned like a toy as the waves grew higher and higher. We all were issued blue padded life vests that we wore all day long. Just as before, each vest had a little battery-operated light fastened to the front. If we were blown over the side and into the sea we were supposed to turn on the red light so they could find us in the ocean. Ha! Who could see us in that foamy, surging, wind-tossed sea, much less throw us a line and pull us back aboard? We would probably have frozen to death in the frigid water anyhow.

The crew struggled valiantly to rig up ropes on deck for us to hold on to. There were barrels stored on the forward deck that broke loose from their moorings and rolled wildly around the deck.

The first night at sea, hundreds of guys got deathly seasick. They were so sick they lost all control of themselves and lay on the floor of the hold. Others lay in their hammocks holding on for dear life as the ship rolled from side to side.

Before we got on board, I steeled myself against the voyage and kept repeating to myself that seasickness is all in your mind and I would not get sick. I was determined not to give in.

To help myself in my vow not to get seasick, I tried to live outside in the cold salt air as much as possible. I slept in my clothes with only my boots removed. As soon as I got awake I pulled on my boots, donned my life vest and woke Joe who had the bunk under me.

The two of us would drop onto the deck which was slippery from all the vomit, and hurriedly climb up the ladder out of the hold. We would both go out on deck for some fresh air until chow time.

The *Rock Hill Victory* was not a large ship and the passage ways were narrow. Two men could not pass each other with life vests on without scraping against each other. It was the same outside on the narrow decks along the sides. We would flatten ourselves against the bulkhead and bend our heads down against the biting wind and freezing rain. It got very uncomfortable as the day wore on and our clothes got wet, but anything was better than that smelly hold. There was no other choice.

Mealtime was a riot. Those of us who managed, by grit or mental attitude, to avoid sickness would show up in the galley, pick up a tray and go down the line to pick up our food. I almost lost it the first morning when breakfast consisted of powdered scrambled eggs, which looked like the stuff back down on the floor of the hold.

As the ship rolled violently, it was a real juggling act to keep your tray from spilling until you could grab a table. Literally, you grabbed a table. Built chest high, the tables were designed so that you ate standing up, there were no seats. Running through the tables from the deck to the ceiling were metal poles which we grabbed and held on to with one hand while we ate with the other, just like on the *Argentina*.

We soon learned to get a spot in the middle of a table instead of one on the end. This was because when the ship rolled from port to starboard, we had to hold on to the poles to keep from falling. Meanwhile the trays all slid to the down side of the ship. During the few moments before the trays all slid in the opposite direction we would eat off the tray that stopped in front of us. The guys on the end would be out of food half of the time.

After a few days of this, the problem lessened because even more GIs succumbed to the sickness and did not show up for meals. We had no wait in line to be fed. Out of 1543 troops on board, one day Joe and I counted only one dozen who made it up for chow.

Each morning the slop on the floor of the hold got deeper. Also the color changed from yellow-orange to yellow-green. One morning an officer came down and tried to get some volunteers to clean up the mess. Joe and I pushed past him and climbed up the ladder. If we had slowed down even to talk about it, we might have been overcome.

I felt so sorry for all those guys who lay in their bunks and looked at us with pleading eyes. "I'll give you five dollars if you can bring me an orange," one GI told me. There were no oranges on board and we could not help them. The head (latrine) was built in to the bow of the ship, which meant it heaved up and down almost constantly. There were men lying all over the deck with their heads lying inside the toilet bowls. Their skin was a pale green and they were so helpless. Only time would cure them.

The ship had a loudspeaker system, and the captain of the ship announced this was the worst storm in the Atlantic in fifty years. One night he announced the ship had recorded a 52 degree roll. We almost went all the way over.

The first day out, the loudspeaker played music. On the second day the man who played the records announced that the table that held the records had rolled over and smashed all of the records except one. It was the Andrews Sisters singing "Rum and Coca-Cola." It played over and over again like a form of Chinese torture. We all learned the words and the tune, which was drummed into our brains. "Rum and Coca-Cola, working for the Yankee dollar." If we could have found the room where the record player was, we would have smashed that record. This was a time before portable radios and tape recorders. All we had were some half size books, which the un-sick GIs read over and over.

Then they issued new Army booklets designed to help us adjust to civilian life. They spent pages telling us how a panel of experts had evaluated all of the military training and experiences and came up with a list of civilian occupations that our training prepared us for. Each of us had an MOS (Military Occupational Specialty) number. I think a rifleman was MOS 720. So we all turned to MOS 720 and looked across the line to see our future career choice. And what had these experts come up with for us? Walrus hunter! Imagine! Not even big game hunter, but walrus hunter! We all screamed laughing and day after day referred to ourselves as Wally the Walrus Hunter. Oh, yes, and jeep drivers were fit to be "truck drivers." How nice.

When we first got aboard, the ship captain announced that he would have us all back in the U.S. by Christmas. That was on December 15th. As the storm raged on, he kept revising his time of arrival date. One night the top of our mast broke off and fell on the deck. Many life boats were smashed into pieces and the large life rafts, which were stored and lashed onto inclined metal frames, went over the side. We consoled ourselves by saying they would not have floated in that turbulent sea anyhow.

As if to tell us that it could be worse, the captain announced one night that the storm was all over the North Atlantic and that another ship ahead of us had lost her rudder and was drifting aimlessly. We started to look out for this ship thinking we might plow into it.

I began to really get scared. One night I saw the steel girders midships across the ship begin to snap. A piece of steel broke off and hit the guy next to me in the forehead. We got him to the sick bay. Joe and I decided to go find the cement patch and see how it was holding. When we found our way to the side hold, there it was. The cement patch was still in the hole in the side of the ship, but water was spraying out from the sides of it all around the patch. Crew members brought huge wooden beams from somewhere and wedged them between the cement block and the opposite bulkhead.

We looked at each other and Joe said, "Court, we better say some more prayers." And we sure did. I prayed to the Lord not to let us die at sea after we had survived the war. I was a lot more scared at sea than I had ever been in combat. On land I could burrow deeper in my foxhole, but out here I was helpless.

Christmas day came and we were still far out to sea. The captain no longer reported estimates of our arrival date in New York. We were finishing breakfast that morning when I heard my name being called over the loudspeaker. I was to report to the office, wherever that was. When I found this little office, I met a chaplain and Rudy Charbonneau, a GI from 3rd Battalion. "Here's the story, Courtney. We have no priest on board and the chaplain here suggested that we could get a Catholic man to lead a rosary service so I chose you. That will be our Christmas since we can't have Mass." I said O.K. and the Protestant chaplain said he would announce on the loudspeaker for the Catholics to assemble in the mess hall.

When I got there the room was full. I pulled out my rosary, we all knelt down, and I led off with the prayers. I happened to kneel down facing the assembly so I was able to see each man's face. I thought about Christmas a year ago in the bombed-out church at Eschdorf. As I looked around, I could see guys from my platoon like Joe Lieb, Joe Puchalski, and Art Schwartz, but then I spotted a guy from K Company whom I had not seen since the Bulge. I was elated to see he was alive. Thank the Lord for this Christmas present. We were alive.

A few days after Christmas, the storm abated and the GIs started to recover from their seasickness. As soon as guys were feeling better and got the floor cleaned and scrubbed, the crap games started. A cardboard box became the backboard and the dice started to roll. Talk about Las Vegas! The games coming over on the *Argentina* were "shoot $50 or $70." These games were "shoot $700 or $800" and real American dollars were on the floor. I had no action, no money. I was a spectator. My ten dollars was spent to buy a case of green leaf candy, a box of Gillette blue blades and four cartons of cigarettes to take home to my brothers. All I could do was suck on my little green candy and observe.

The games were on the floor of the big hold. Guys were hanging out of hammocks to watch. Participants were on the floor holding big wads of money. One guy shot $800 and rolled boxcars, a loser. He kept the dice and said, "shoot $800." He was covered quickly, and he again rolled boxcars, a loser. He got red faced and yelled, "shoot $800!" a third time. He was covered, and he rolled snake eyes (1 and 1), another loser. He was now down $2,400 and feeling very depressed. Each time he shot the dice, there was a short, fat little guy with black curly hair who would scream, "When do I get my turn at the dice?" in a high squeaky voice.

The big loser, who was feeling mad and frustrated but still had control of the dice, yelled, "O.K. Here, you want your turn, go ahead and shoot."

The little guy grabbed the dice and squealed, "Now we'll see some action! Here we go!" He shook the dice over his head and yelled, "Come to Papa!"

"Hold it!" the crowd shouted.

The big loser said, "You haven't put any money down yet. What are you going to shoot?" The other guys grunted, "Yeah! Where's your money?"

The little guy opened his hand and carefully unwrapped two very crumpled one dollar bills and laid them on the floor. "Shoot $2!" he said.

With that the players revolted and started to chase the little guy, who had grabbed back his two dollars and ran to climb the ladder up out of the hold. Our last view of him was as he was about two rungs above the big loser who was closing fast behind him red faced and screaming. Without any pause, the crap game continued as the little guy had left the dice on the floor.

On the night of December 28th, we arrived in New York Harbor. We were all excited and crammed the bow to see all the lights of the port. We thought we would land that night, but to our dismay a crewman came forward and released the anchor chair. Clunk! We stayed in the lower harbor all night.

The next day we finally started to move again, this time in a downpour of rain. It was so rainy and misty that we could barely see the *Statue of Liberty* as we passed her. I looked up at the Lady and said, "Old girl, if you ever want to see me again you will have to turn around." I had already promised myself I would never go on an ocean boat trip again.

Our excitement built as we got off the ship and onto a ferryboat. Our eyes lit up at the sight of advertising posters on the walls of the boat. Big red and white ads for Kessler's whiskey! Wow! Real American advertising. We did not realize that we had missed it. Bernie McKittrick's grin covered his whole face and Ron McGregor, said "We are really back in the U.S.A."

We all joked that there was no band to greet us or pretty girls. We saw one sign of "Well Done" on the roof of a pier but it was faded and the paint peeled off. It seemed that the first troops home were the ones closest to the French coast and we were the farthest ones in eastern Europe. *C'est la Guerre!*

Then we piled onto real American railroad coaches and sat on green padded seats and looked out the windows as we rolled across New Jersey. "Look, there goes a car! Look, there's a Sunoco station!" We were like little kids seeing America for the first time.

We were a jovial gang as we unloaded on the siding at Fort Dix, New Jersey, and carried our duffel bags to our barracks area. We were still the 26th Yankee Division, and we were pleased to see that each barracks had our YD and unit designation in letters over each front door.

As soon as we chose a bunk and dropped our gear, we asked the cadre corporal where the nearest public phones were. He told us and we made a wild dash out the door and across the lot to the phones. There was already a line at each booth, but no one talked long because in those days we were all trained at home that long distance calls cost money and not to talk past the three minute minimum. My dad used to hold up his fingers to tell us when we had one minute left.

How great it was to hear my mother and dad's voices on the phone. Of course they wanted to know how soon I could get home, but I didn't know. Brother Bill, now a captain, was home from the Pacific and my brother John was home from Texas. I would be the last brother home from the war.

The next day we were processed to become civilians. More record checks and physicals. They discovered after all this time that I never had an X-ray when I enlisted, so I had to get one before I could leave the Army.

Later we were herded into a large theater where a major gave us all a pep talk about joining the reserves. His big selling point was that we would be able to maintain our present rank if we ever had to come back onto active duty. "Ha!" I said, "I won't have any trouble keeping my rank as a Pfc.!" and I headed for the exit. You guys may only go 24 hours ahead of me as reservists if we ever have to come back in, but I'll take the 24 hours.

That night in the PX, Joe Puchalski bought me beer since I had no money and we had not been paid yet. We reminisced about the days in the E.T.O. and talked about how good it would be to finally get home. Joe had a son, Vince, he was excited to see plus his wife, Sue.

They really did not fool around at Fort Dix and processed us out pretty fast. We boarded a train for Pennsylvania early one afternoon. Here is where we said good-bye to the YD. We had been split up into groups to head out for discharge centers such as Massachusetts (the home of the 26th Division), Florida, and Texas.

When I said good-bye to Sam Harper, I asked him what he was going to do when he got back home to the Everglades. He said he was going to start up a still again and sell moonshine. I said, "Sam, you don't want to go back into the chain gang do you? What if you are caught?" He said, "No way. I learned a lot in the Army. I learned how to camouflage." I laughed. It was a sad parting as we pulled away from guys we had lived with for two years or more.

It was New Year's Eve when we arrived at the railhead at Indiantown Gap Military Reservation near Harrisburg, Pennyslvania. In the darkness, we loaded onto semitrailers that took us up the hill to the barracks. No wild driver on this trip.

When we got into our barracks a sergeant came in and shouted, "Anyone who wants to leave just take off! No passes! No questions!

Just take off, but be back tomorrow by 8:00 a.m."

There was a rumble as a lot of guys left. Joe, Ron, and I decided we could not get home and get back in one night so we just stayed put. When we found the PX, Joe bought the beer again. He was a great guy. I told them about New Year's Eve two years before when I had arrived at Camp Campbell, Kentucky, to join the YD, and here I was back in Pennsylvania not too far from Altoona.

On New Year's Day we got processed some more, and by now they had handled so many outgoing GIs that they had it down pat. I remember Joe Lieb saying how they even had an X marked on the counter and a sign saying Put Your Elbow Here, to take your blood pressure.

We went through a big room where we were issued any uniform items we were missing. It seemed strange to be issued new items when we were getting discharged. There was a row of sewing machines humming away as women sewed a "ruptured duck" onto the left breast of our Ike jackets. This was a gold bird with a broken wing to symbolize that we were in uniform but no longer soldiers. We also received a gold ruptured duck pin to place on our civilian clothes to show we were veterans.

We had supper and one more night at the PX before our big day. I called home collect again and told my folks I expected to be discharged the next day and I would come home on the first train I could get out of Harrisburg.

The next day was bright and sunny, January 2, 1946. After breakfast we went through a pay line and collected mustering out pay of $100. I was excited to see a window with a red and gold sign over it that read Pennsylvania Railroad Ticket Office. I bought my one way ticket to Altoona and was told I could probably make the 3:00 p.m. train.

We were assigned to groups of about fifty men to be processed since we were no longer in YD units. Our group waited outside the little military church for another group to be discharged. Soon the group of GIs came out of the church smiling broadly.

Our turn was next as we filed in and took our seats. We were given a very fine talk by a major who told us we had done our duty for our country. We had fought for it, and now we should go home and be an active part of it. I remember how he told us to get involved and participate in the affairs of our home towns. He said it was up to all of us to continue to make America great. Everyone there sat up a little straighter as he finished. We were proud to be Americans.

"And now, what you have all been waiting for. As I call your name please come forward to pick up your discharge papers." A lieutenant read off the names and we each went forward. I was grinning broadly as the major handed me my Honorable Discharge. He shook hands and said, "Congratulations, Mister."

After the last man received his discharge and returned to his seat, the major asked us all to rise, stand at attention and, "For the last time men," salute as they played the "*Star Spangled Banner.*" At the end we all had lumps in our throats. The major said, "Dismissed. Good-bye, men."

What a feeling! At long last we were out of the Army. No one could tell us what to do anymore. We were told we could eat lunch at the mess hall, but no one did. We headed for the buses to go into Harrisburg.

It was early afternoon when the bus dropped us off at the Pennsylvania Railroad Station on Market Street. About six of us walked around the corner to a little cafe to get a sandwich and a beer. We watched the clock move slowly toward 3:00 P.M. As we stepped out of the cafe, we stopped to watch the Harrisburg traffic and to admire the cars. Here we were, in a real American city!

We all gathered together in the same coach and the train pulled out for the west. McKittrick, Joe Lieb, and Harold Nixdorf were heading to Pittsburgh along with Ron McGregor who was going home to Yatesboro. Jake Lipps had left earlier for Bradford and Joe Puchalski took a Greyhound bus to Scranton.

We were counting the miles as we neared Huntington when suddenly we heard a cracking sound, and the train came to a stop. We sat there for a long time before we learned from the conductor that our car had broken a wheel, and the train had to wait until a crew came and replaced it.

Holy Cow! So close to home and now the train broke down. It seemed that everyone and everything was conspiring against our return to our families.

At 7:30 P.M., in the dark, an hour and a half late, we steamed at last into the station at Altoona. I picked up my bag and for the last time shook hands all around with my platoon mates. We wished each other well, and I stepped out on the platform just in time to hear my brother John yell, "Hey, Bill, here he is!" My brother Bill was checking the next car door to try to find me, and he hurried over as I stepped off the train. John, Bill, and I shook hands as Bill explained that he was leaving on the same train to go back to his job at Youngstown, Ohio. I said good-bye to him and told him to turn left and get in the car with my squad and meet the guys. Just then my brothers Bob and Don arrived and we shook hands and yelled to each other in our excitement. Dad and Mother reached us next, and I hugged them both.

John said, "I'll take your duffel bag. The car is up this way."

Dad said, "Put your overcoat on. It's cold here."

We all piled into Dad's 1939 Oldsmobile and drove up the hills of snow to 1411 19th Avenue, our three-story home. We were all trying to talk at once we were so jubilant and excited.

I carried my bag into the house and set it down on the living room floor for the last time. I looked around and said, "Thank God. The war is really over and I made it home."

Afterword

When I entered the Army right out of high school, I left a sheltered life and was somewhat lacking in self-confidence. I was afraid to try anything very physical like climbing over a wall.

After the war, I came home full of confidence. I could handle anything. I had survived combat, and I learned that it is not your physical prowess but your inner courage that counts.

Millions of American GIs came home with this same confidence, which translated into the powerful thrust and growth of our nation in the late 1940s and 1950s. We had the expansion of colleges, new businesses, new homes, a mobile society rearing families and feeling pride in our country.

We must never forget that freedom is not free. We have to fight to keep it from tyrants. Some must die so that the rest of us can enjoy our free life.

How is our nation's moral future today? Would we unite as we did in World War II? Would our young men be willing to endure the rigors of combat? Would the civilian population sacrifice and do without luxuries, accept rationing, and more taxes?

Even in peacetime we must always keep our military strong. Future wars may not allow us time to train and equip the military as we did in World War II.

I learned why young men make the best soldiers. They have fewer responsibilities, no family to worry about, and have youthful optimism, a spirit of adventure, and a feeling of immortality.

I also learned that men of religious faith have stronger lives and can accept hardship and danger where men of no faith can be consumed with fear.

My faith in Jesus Christ as my Lord was tested in fire and only made stronger. Praise the Lord.

Glossary

Statistics

Index

Glossary

A & P: ammunition & pioneer

Ack-ack: antiaircraft artillery

Amis: German nickname for American soldiers

Ammo: ammunition

APO: Army Post Office

ASTP: Army Specialized Training Program

AT: antitank

Barracks bag: a heavy cloth duffel bag

BBC: British Broadcasting Corporation

Bouncing Betty: German land mine that bounced up in the air about three feet and then exploded sideways to inflict maximum damage on personnel

Cat-Eyes: small, green lights the size of a cat's eyes mounted on the front and rear of Army vehicles for night driving

CG: Commanding General

Chow: a meal

CO: Commanding Officer

CP: Command Post

CQ: Charge of Quarters

C-ration: a small can of food for one person. C-rations consisted of one can which contained crackers, candy, lemon powder, or coffee. The other can contained precooked food such as meat and beans.

Croix de Guerre: Cross of War, a French military decoration

DE: destroyer escort, a naval vessel

Dogface: nickname for common frontline infantrymen

DP: displaced person

DUKW or DUCKS: $2\frac{1}{2}$-ton trucks equipped with propellers that ran on water and then had wheels to drive up on beaches

Eighty-eight (88): German artillery piece that fired 88 mm shell

Epaulet: shoulder strap on a military uniform

ETO: European Theater of Operations

Fifty-seven (57): American antitank guns that fired 57 mm shells

FO: forward observer

Fraulein: German word meaning young girl

GI: government issue, loosely used as nickname for American soldiers, or any item issued by the Army, or any military policy or rule

Goldbrick: a term used to denote any soldier who avoided work or duty

HE: high explosive, as artillery shells

Highball: Army slang for salute

Jeep: Army slang for general purpose (GP) military vehicle

KP: kitchen police; workers in kitchen or mess hall

K-ration: Army field ration in a small box, consisting of one small can of food such as cheese, plus crackers, cigarettes, candy, or toilet paper

Latrine: Army toilet, or slit-trench dug for such a purpose

LCVP: landing craft vehicle personnel; used to land troops on beach

Leggings: canvas wrappers that laced around the leg from the shoe to the knee, later replaced with combat boots

Luftwaffe: German Air Force

ME-109: Messerschmitt, German fighter plane

Mess hall: military dining hall

M-1: basic Army .30 caliber semiautomatic rifle

MOS: Military Occupational Specialty (job description)

MP: Military Police

Musette bag: a canvas bag for personal effects with straps to attach to a tank

Non-com: short for non-commissioned officer such as corporal or sergeant

OD: olive drab

P-47: American fighter aircraft

Platoon: an Army unit consisting of two or more squads of men

POE: port of embarkation

Potato masher: slang for German hand grenade

POW: prisoner of war

PRR: Pennsylvania Railroad Company

PX: Post Exchange, general store for the military

Rednose: cowl of P-47 fighter planes were painted red by the 8th Air Force

Retreat: Army ceremony to lower the flag daily at 5:00 P.M.

Round: one bullet or shell

Ruble: unit of Russian currency
Schilling: unit of Austrian currency
Screaming GIs: slang for diarrhea
Shock troops: specially trained troops for assault purposes
SNAFU: acronym for situation normal, all fouled up
Sous-Lieutenant: French second lieutenant
SSO: Special Services Officer
TD: tank destroyer
TOT: time on target
U-boat: German submarine so named because they were always numbered with a "U" prefix
WWI: World War I
WWII: World War II
YD: Yankee Division

Statistics

Total days in combat:

Division	210 days
328th Infantry Regiment	180 days
104th Infantry Regiment	177 days
101st Infantry Regiment	166 days

Battle stars:

1. Northern France (7–14 September 1944)
2. The Rhineland (6 October–12 December 1944; 28 January–23 March 1945)
3. Ardennes (20 December 1944–28 January 1945)
4. Central Europe (24 March–8 May 1945)

Prisoners captured:

221,501

Decorations:

Medal of Honor	1
Distinguished Service Cross	37
Distinguished Service Cross Oak Leaf Cluster	1
Legion of Merit	5
Silver Star	879
Silver Star Oak Leaf Cluster	24
Soldier's Medal	27
Bronze Star Medal	4,788
Bronze Star Medal Oak Leaf Cluster	295
Air Medal	33
Air Medal Oak Leaf Cluster	56
Purple Heart	2,779
Purple Heart Oak Leaf Cluster	401
Grand Total	9,296

Total casualties:

18,950 officers and men

Source: *History of a Combat Regiment, 1639–1945: 104th Infantry* (1945)

Index

RICHARD D. COURTNEY was born the seventh child in a family of nine and raised at the family home in Altoona, Pennsylvania. After the war, he started with Bell Telephone Company of Pennsylvania at Harrisburg as a salesman. In a thirteen-year career, he advanced to sales manager for central Pennsylvania, then to manager of the Wilkes-Barre District, and finally to headquarters of Philadelphia where he coordinated company marketing activities for Pennsylvania and Delaware. In 1959, he resigned to found a food and vending service in Muncie, Indiana, with his brother Bob, which they later merged into a national corporation. Married to Constance Wool at Williamsport, Pennsylvania, in 1955, he and his wife raised six sons and one daughter. Now retired, they still reside in Muncie.